Let's Get Musical

Year 7-9 Teacher's Guide

Chris Gill

Copyright © 2017 by Chris Gill

All rights reserved. No part of this publication may be reproduced, distributed, or transmitted in any form or by any means, including photocopying, recording, or other electronic or mechanical methods, without the prior written permission of the publisher.

First edition: September 2017

ABOUT THE AUTHOR

Chris Gill has a Bachelor of Music from the University of Birmingham and a Postgraduate Certificate of Education in Secondary Music from University College Worcester. He has twenty years' experience in teaching music in both the independent and state sectors, and is currently Director of Music at Rye St Antony, Oxford. He has also worked as a freelance conductor and is the founder and chairman of Heritage Opera.

www.chrisgill.co.uk

Let's Get Musical
a complete classroom music course for ages 11-16

Let's Get Musical – Year 8 Workbook
Let's Get Musical – Year 8 Workbook
Let's Get Musical – Year 9 Workbook
Let's Get Musical – Years 7-9 Teacher's Guide
Let's Get Musical – GCSE Workbook for the 9-1 Edexcel Exam

www.letsgetmusical.co.uk

The website contains links for purchasing copies and media links for the lessons.

Other books by Chris Gill

Harmonising Bach Chorales
The Heritage Opera Guide

Contents

Year 7 10
   Elements of Music 11
      Objective 11
      Lesson overview 11
      Subject-specific vocabulary 11
      Assessments 11
      Lesson 1 – Rhythm 12
      Lesson 2 – Pitch 14
      Lesson 3 – Texture 15
      Lesson 4 – Tempo and Dynamics 16
      Lesson 5 – Structure 17
      Lesson 6 – Composing 19
      Lesson 7 – Instruments 20
      Lesson 8 - Conclusion 22
      Extra Activity: Musical Happy Families 24
      Picture credits 27
   Rock 'n' Roll 28
      Objectives 28
      Lesson Overview 28
      Subject-specific vocabulary 28
      Assessments 28
      Lesson 1: The Origins of Rock 'n' Roll 29
      Lesson 2: The 12-Bar Blues 30
      Lesson 3: The Bass Line 32
      Lesson 4: The I-vi-IV-V Progression 33
      Lesson 5: Preparing Group Arrangement 34
      Lesson 6: Group performances and listening exercise 35
      Extension/cover work 36
      Listening to Rock 'n' Roll 37
      Hound Dog 37
      Listening to Rock 'n' Roll ANSWERS 38
      Hound Dog 38

Rock 'n' Roll: Assessment Sheet 39

The Beatles 40

Objectives 40

Lesson Overview 40

Subject-specific vocabulary 40

Assessments 40

Lesson 1: Love Me Do 41

Lesson 2: Eleanor Rigby 43

Lesson 3: Can't Buy Me Love 45

Lesson 4: Let it Be 47

Lesson 5: Arranging a Beatles song 48

Lesson 6: Performing a Beatles song 49

The Beatles: Assessment Sheet 50

Baroque Music 51

Objectives 51

Lesson overview 51

Vocabulary 51

Assessment 51

Lesson 1 - Pachelbel's *Canon* 52

Lesson 2 - Scarlatti's Sonata 54

Lesson 3 - Bach's Toccata and Fugue 55

Lesson 4 – Handel's Messiah 56

Lesson 5 - Purcell's Dido and Aeneas 58

Lesson 6 - Vivaldi's Four Seasons 59

Lessons 7/8: Group composition and performance 60

Baroque Music: Assessment Sheet 61

African Music 62

Objectives 62

Lesson overview 62

Vocabulary 62

Assessment 62

Lesson 1: Wimmoweh 63

Lesson 2: African instruments 65

Lesson 3: African Rhythms 67

Lesson 4: Group composition 68

Lesson 5: Singing African Songs 69

    Lesson 6: Listening to African Music ... 70

    Listening to African Music: answers ... 71

    AFRICA FORESTDANCE PERFORM SOSISA ... 71

    African Music: assessment sheet ... 72

Year 8 ... 73

Film Music ... 74

    Objectives ... 74

    Overview ... 74

    Subject-specific vocabulary ... 74

    Assessments ... 74

    Lesson 1 – Film and Genre ... 75

    Lesson 2 – Musical Ideas for Film Genres ... 76

    Lesson 3 – Orchestral Film Music ... 77

    Lesson 4 – Listening to the James Bond Theme ... 78

    Lesson 5 – Practising the James Bond Theme ... 79

    Lesson 6 – Performing the James Bond Theme ... 80

    Lesson 7 – Composing Film Music ... 81

    Lesson 8 – Final evaluation ... 83

    Film Music: assessment sheet ... 84

Caribbean Music ... 85

    Objectives ... 85

    Lesson Overview ... 85

    Subject-specific vocabulary ... 85

    Assessments ... 85

    Lesson 1: Calypso ... 86

    Lesson 2: Yellow Bird ... 87

    Lesson 3: Three Little Chords ... 88

    Lesson 4: Riffs ... 89

    Lesson 5: Three Little Birds ... 90

    Lesson 6: Caribbean Music ... 91

    Caribbean Music Assessment Sheet ... 92

Indian Music ... 93

    Objectives ... 93

    Lesson overview ... 93

    Vocabulary ... 93

    Assessment ... 93

Lesson 1: Instruments 94
Lesson 2: Ragas 95
Lesson 3: Composing a raga 96
Lesson 4: Playing your raga 97
Lesson 5: Talas 98
Lesson 6: Further listening 99
Listening to Indian Music 100
Indian Music: assessment sheet 101

Classical Music 102
Objectives 102
Lesson Overview 102
Subject-specific vocabulary 102
Assessments 102
Lesson 1: Schubert's 'The Trout' and Strophic Form 103
Lesson 2: Gluck's 'What is life' and Rondo form 105
Lesson 3: Consolidation of Classical Vocal Music 107
Lesson 4: Haydn's 'Emperor Quartet' and Variation form 108
Lesson 5: Mozart's Minuet and Ternary Form 109
Lesson 6: Consolidation of musical forms 111
Lesson 7: Beethoven's Fifth Symphony and Sonata Form 113
Lesson 8: Conclusion 115

Mozart's Minuet 121
Sonata Form: a musical jigsaw 122
Classical Music Listening Exercise 123
Answers 125
Sonata form jigsaw 125
Listening Exercise 125
Classical Music: Assessment Sheet 126

Jazz 127
Objectives 127
Lesson outline 127
Subject-specific vocabulary 127
Assessments 128
Lesson 1 – Blues and Ragtime 129
Lesson 2 – New Orleans Jazz 130
Lesson 3 – The Swing Era 131

- Lesson 4 – Later Jazz Styles 133
- Lesson 5 – When the Saints go Marching In 134
- Lesson 6 – Improvising Assessment 135
- Jazz – Assessment Sheet 136

Year 9 137

Dance Music 138
- Objectives 138
- Lesson Overview 138
- Subject-specific vocabulary 138
- Assessments 138
- Lesson 1: Metre 139
- Lesson 2: Instruments 141
- Lesson 3: Disco 142
- Lesson 4: Interim Assessment 144
- Lessons 5: Performing/Composing 145
- Lessons 6-8: Performing/Composing 146

Gamelan 147
- Objectives 147
- Lesson Overview 147
- Subject-specific vocabulary 147
- Assessments 147
- Lesson 1: Introducing the Gamelan 148
- Lesson 2: Performing Gamelan Music 149
- Lesson 3: Extending the performance *(optional)* 150
- Lesson 4: Composing for the gamelan 151
- Lesson 5: Performing and evaluating compositions 152

Minimalism 153
- Objectives 153
- Lesson Overview 153
- Subject-specific vocabulary 153
- Assessments 153
- Lesson 1 – Motif and Ostinato 154
- Lesson 2 – Note Addition and Note Subtraction 155
- Lesson 3 – Canon and Layering 156
- Lesson 4 – Augmentation and Diminution 158
- Lesson 5 – Phasing and Phase-Shifting 160

- Lesson 6: Class Composition/Performance 'in C' 162
- Minimalism: Assessment Sheet 164

Latin Music 165
- Objectives 165
- Lesson overview 165
- Subject-specific vocabulary 165
- Assessments 165
- Lesson 1 – Listening to Samba 166
- Lesson 2 – Performing a Samba 168
- Lesson 3 - Listening to Tangos 169
- Lesson 4 – Performing a Tango 170
- Lesson 5 – Composing a Tango: chords and bass line 171
- Lesson 6 – Composing a Tango: melody 172
- Latin Music: Assessment Sheet 173
- Picture credits 174

Romantic Music 175
- Objectives 175
- Lesson Overview 175
- Subject-specific vocabulary 175
- Assessments 175
- Lesson 1: Romantic Music 176
- Lesson 2: Oom-pah-pah 177
- Lesson 3: The 'Minute' waltz 178
- Lesson 4: A symphonic waltz 179
- Lesson 5: An operatic waltz 180
- Lesson 6: Listening to Programme Music 181
- Lessons 7/8 – Composing Programme Music 182
- Romantic Music: Assessment Sheet 183
- Picture credits 184
- Chopin's 'Minute' Waltz 184

Gospel, Blues and Soul 185
- Objectives 185
- Lesson Overview 185
- Subject-specific vocabulary 185
- Assessments 185
- Lesson 1 – Two Spirituals 186

Lesson 2: Gospel Music 188
Lesson 3: Rhythm 'n' Blues 190
Lesson 4: The Birth of Soul 191
Lesson 5: Respect 192
Lesson 6: Stand By Me 193
Lessons 7-8 – Group arrangement/performance 194
Gospel, Blues and Soul: Assessment Sheet 196
Picture credits 197

Year 7

Elements of Music
Rock 'n' Roll
The Beatles
Baroque Music
African Music

Elements of Music

Key Stage 3 Scheme of Work (8 lessons)

Objective

- To become familiar with the seven elements of music (pitch, rhythm, dynamics, tempo, timbre, texture, structure) through performing, composing and listening

Lesson overview

1. Rhythm
2. Pitch
3. Texture
4. Tempo and Dynamics
5. Structure
6. Composing
7. Instruments
8. Conclusion

Subject-specific vocabulary

- Rhythm - crotchets, quavers, dotted crotchets and minims
- Pitch – higher, lower, range, step, leap, phrase, melodic shape
- Texture – monophonic, homophonic, polyphonic, heterophonic
- Tempo - Allegro – fast, Allegretto – quite fast, Moderato – medium, Andante – walking pace, Lento – slow, accelerando (accel.) – getting faster, ritardando (rit.) – get slower
- Dynamics - fortissimo (ff) – very loud, forte (f) – loud, mezzo-forte (mf) – medium loud, mezzo piano (mp) –medium soft, Piano (p) – soft, Pianissimo (pp) – very soft, crescendo (cresc.) – getting louder, diminuendo (dim.) – getting softer
- Structure – phrases A, B, C etc.
- Instruments – plucked/bowed strings, woodwind, brass, pitched/unpitched, percussion, others
- Performing, Composing and Listening

Assessments

- Performing – keyboard performance of 'Ode to Joy'
- Composing – keyboard piece using six elements of music
- Listening – Rhythmic and melodic dictation; exercises on texture, structure and instruments

Lesson 1 – Rhythm

Objective
- To differentiate between long and short notes (crotchets, quavers, dotted crotchets and minims)

Resources
- Whiteboard and marker
- Pupils' workbooks and pencils

Procedure

Starter – composing own name rhythms (10 minutes)
- Pupils stand in a circle and march on spot to create steady pulse.
- In turn they say their first name and surname in the space of exactly four beats each. The teacher explains that this is a RHYTHM.
- The pupils clap the rhythm of their names as they say them, then without saying their names.

Main 1 – performing other name rhythms (15 minutes)
- The teacher chooses 5 pupils from the register whose names all have different four-beat rhythms. The pupils stand in a line at the front of the class facing the rest of the pupils. The teacher writes the pupils' first names and surnames on the whiteboard, separating the syllables with dashes. The rest of the class chant the names in order, trying to make the names as rhythmic as possible.
- The teacher writes the four-beat rhythm for each name above the name using a combination of crotchets, quavers, dotted crotchets and minims, explaining what a rhythm is and how long each note is. The rest of the class claps and chants the names simultaneously.
- The teacher rubs out the names, but leaves the rhythms on the whiteboard. The five chosen pupils sit down with the rest of the class. The whole class claps the rhythms in order.
- The teacher numbers the rhythms 1-5. The teacher holds up 1-5 fingers and counts the class in '1-2-3-4'. The class should then clap the correct rhythm.
- The teacher repeats the previous step with individual pupils.

Main 2 – listening to other name rhythms (20 minutes)
- The teacher explains that the pupils are going to play a game where they identify the correct rhythm 10 times. First, there is a practice. The teacher claps twice one of the 5 rhythms on the board. The pupils hold up, in front of their chests, the correct number of fingers (1-5) for the clapped rhythm.
- Repeat the previous step 5 times, this time with the pupils scoring 1 for the correct rhythm (first time) and 0 for the incorrect rhythm. They keep their score in their head.
- The teacher announces that rhythms 6-10 will be based on *two* rhythms (which could be the same). The teacher claps the two rhythms without a gap between them. This time, the pupils have to hold up *two* hands to show the correct rhythm. They score 2 if both hands are correct, 1 if one hand is correct, or 0 if neither are correct.
- At the end of the game, the teacher asks pupils' scores out of 15.

Plenary – rhythmic dictation (15 minutes)

- The teacher distributes workbooks – pupils name their books on page 1 then turn to listening exercise on page 2. Teacher claps each rhythm (including the example twice). The pupils write down the rhythm and hand them in for marking at the end of the lesson.

TEACHER'S COPY for clapping and marking

Year 7 - Elements of Music
Rhythmic Dictation

13

Lesson 2 – Pitch

Objective
- All pupils differentiate between high and low notes
- Many pupils identify whether one note is higher, lower or the same as another
- Some pupils identify the melodic shape of a short conjunct phrase

Resources
- Pupils' workbooks
- Keyboards and headphones

Procedure

Starter – Chanting and singing 'Ode to Joy' (10 minutes)
- Pupils copy the teacher chant the English words for 'Ode to Joy', noting the rhythms
- Pupils learn to sing the melody of 'Ode to Joy'

Main 1 – Pitch dictation – listening (20 minutes)
- On page 3 of workbooks, pupils write out the melody played or sung by the teacher one bar at a time, by working out whether each note is higher than, lower than or the same as the previous one. The melody should stay within the range of the five notes CDEFG given at the top of the sheet
- Pupils should note that the melody is mostly made up of steps (the few leaps are already given on the sheet). The melody also has a recognisable shape if the 'dots' were to be joined: for example, the 1st, 2nd and 4th phrases all go smoothly up, down, up and down
- Pupils should copy the rhythms, using crotchets, dotted crotchets, quavers and minims
- When finished, pupils check their work with the printed melody on page 4 of workbook

Main 2 – Performing on the keyboard (20 minutes)
- In pairs, pupils learn to play the melody (right hand only) of 'Ode to Joy' with their right hand from page 4 of workbook
- More advanced pupils can start to learn the left hand as well

Plenary – Performing on the keyboard (10 minutes)
- Some pupils perform their work-in-progress to the rest of the class

Lesson 3 – Texture

Objectives
- All pupils differentiate between a single melodic line and more than one line
- Some pupils identify whether the texture is single melody, melody and accompaniment or several melodies
- A few pupils use subject-specific words to describe texture: monophonic, homophonic, polyphonic or heterophonic

Resources
- Pupils' workbooks
- 6-minute video about Musical Texture: https://www.youtube.com/watch?v=_J2R20X16Jc
- Musical Texture quiz playlist: https://www.youtube.com/playlist?list=PLnvmFAu748V58ihHKDwFkG6kyXwxNvtQ4

Procedure

Starter – listening to texture in 'Ode to Joy' (10 minutes)
- Teacher plays through 'Ode to Joy' with both hands. Pupils answer the question: 'What has been added to the melody since last lesson?' (Notes in the left hand.) The teacher explains that this is a change in TEXTURE.
- Teacher plays 'Ode to Joy' with both hands again. This time, pupils are encouraged by the teacher describe the TEXTURE of each 4-bar phrase along these lines:
    1. single melodic line   2. another version of the melody played at the same time
    3. two tunes together   4. melody and accompaniment

Main 1 – listening to different textures (20 minutes)
- Pupils watch and listen to 6-minute video about Musical Texture, learning about different kinds of texture: monophonic, homophonic, polyphonic and heterophonic ('biphonic' is also covered, but this can be ignored for the purposes of this lesson)
- Pupils complete Musical Texture quiz on page 6 of workbooks. Answers as follows:
    1. Gregorian chant - monophonic
    2. Lonesome valley - heterophonic
    3. Carmen overture - homophonic
    4. Bach cello suite – monophonic
    5. Shostakovich fugue - polyphonic
    6. Indian classical music - heterophonic
    7. Unomathemba - homophonic
    8. Don't Be So Hard on Yourself - homophonic

Main 2 – performing 'Ode to Joy' with different textures (20 minutes)
- Pupils practise as much of 'Ode to Joy' from page 4 of workbooks as they can with the (increasingly challenging) variety of textures provided by the left hand. If they are not able to play hands together at all, they should continue to practise the right hand melody by itself.

Plenary – performing 'Ode to Joy' with different textures (10 minutes)
- One or two pupils play each of the four phrases of 'Ode to Joy', thus demonstrating the different textures (monophonic, heterophonic, polyphonic and homophonic)

Lesson 4 – Tempo and Dynamics

Objectives
- All pupils differentiate between fast/slow and loud/soft
- Most pupils identify gradual changes in tempo and dynamics: getting faster/slower, louder/softer
- Some pupils use Italian words to describe tempo and dynamics

Resources
- 'In the Hall of the Mountain King' https://www.youtube.com/watch?v=xrIYT-MrVaI
- Keyboards (one between two)
- Sheet music for 'Ode to Joy'

Procedure

Starter – Listening to tempo and dynamics (5 minutes)
- Teacher plays 'In the Hall of the Mountain King'. What changes occur during the piece? (It gradually becomes faster and louder.)

Main 1 – Understanding tempo and dynamics (10 minutes)
- On page 7 of workbooks, pupils write five Italian words for tempo in order from slow to fast
- Pupils discuss and write down the meaning of 'accelerando' and 'ritardando'
- Pupils work out what the dynamic markings (pp-ff) signify
- Pupils discuss and write down the meaning of 'crescendo' and 'diminuendo'
- The following musical terms are used on page 7 of the workbook:
    - TEMPO Allegro – fast, Allegretto – quite fast, Moderato – medium, Andante – walking pace, Lento – slow, accelerando (accel.) – getting faster, ritardando (rit.) – get slower
    - DYNAMICS fortissimo (ff) – very loud, forte (f) – loud, mezzo-forte (mf) – medium loud, mezzo piano (mp) – medium soft, Piano (p) – soft, Pianissimo (pp) – very soft, crescendo (cresc.) – getting louder, diminuendo (dim.) – getting softer

Main 2 – Performing on the keyboard with tempo and dynamics (25 minutes)
- Pupils practise as much of 'Ode to Joy' as they can with the (increasingly challenging) variety of textures provided by the left hand. If they are not able to play hands together at all, they should continue to practise the right hand melody by itself.

Plenary - performing 'Ode to Joy' with tempo and dynamics (20 minutes)
- All pupils play as much of 'Ode to Joy' as they are able, incorporating the differences in pitch, rhythm, texture, tempo and dynamics
- Teacher assesses the keyboard performance

Lesson 5 – Structure

Objectives

- All pupils recognise repetition and contrast in a piece of music
- Most pupils identify the phrase structure of a section of music (e.g. AABA)
- Some pupils identify slight variations in repeated phrases (e.g. AA_1BA_1)

Resources

- Pupils' workbooks
- Piano
- Coldplay – 'Clocks' https://www.youtube.com/watch?v=d020hcWA_Wg
- 'Down by the Salley Gardens' (Irish folk song) https://www.youtube.com/watch?v=027ZJX5XVjs
- 'The Elephant' from *The Carnival of the Animals* by Saint-Saëns https://www.youtube.com/watch?v=VZAGLJtj5RU

Procedure

Starter: Listening to the phrase structure in 'Ode to Joy' (10 minutes)

- Teacher (or confident pupil) plays the right-hand melody of 'Ode to Joy' on the piano while the pupils follow the score. Which phrases are more or less the same? (The 1st, 2nd and 4th.) Which one is different? (The 3rd.) Are there any slight differences in the similar phrases? (Yes – the last bar of the 1st phrase is different from the last bar of the 2nd and 4th phrase. The 1st phrase feels 'unfinished' but the 2nd and 4th phrases feel 'finished'.)
- Teacher explains that the STRUCTURE of a piece can be described by giving each phrase a letter of the alphabet starting with A, using the same letter for similar phrases and the next letter in the alphabet for different phrases. 'Ode to Joy' can be described as having the structure AABA. (An even more detailed description is AA_1BA_1, because of the slight variations between the A sections.)

Main 1: Listening to the phrase structure in other pieces (10 minutes)

- On page 8 of workbooks, pupils identify the phrase structure in the first section of the following pieces (disregarding the introductions):
  - Coldplay – 'Clocks' (AAAA)
  - 'Down by the Salley Gardens' (Irish folk song) (AABA)
  - 'The Elephant' from *The Carnival of the Animals* by Saint-Saëns (ABA_1C)

Main 2: Composing a melody using a chosen structure (30 minutes)

- Pupils now begin composing their keyboard piece for their music exam on page 10 of their workbooks. Using 'Ode to Joy' as a model, the piece should have the following:
  - RHYTHM: melody uses crotchets, dotted crotchets, quavers and minims
  - PITCH: melody uses the notes CDEFG; mainly stepwise; recognisable shape
  - STRUCTURE: Four four-bar phrases in 4/4 time; A clear phrase structure that has both repetition and contrast

Plenary – Performing composition on the keyboard (10 minutes)

- Some pupils play their work-in-progress to the rest of the class (if they prefer, the teacher can play it). Does their piece have all the features listed above?

Lesson 6 – Composing

Objectives

- All pupils compose a piece of music showing some variety in the elements of music
- Most pupils compose a piece showing a variety of rhythm, pitch, texture, tempo, dynamics and structure
- Some pupils exploit the elements of music in a subtle and expressive way, for example with a slight variation in melody or a well-placed crescendo

Resources

- 'Ode to Joy' sheet music (one per pupil)
- Composition worksheet (one per pupil)
- Keyboards and headphones

Procedure

Starter – Listening to six elements of music in 'Ode to Joy' (5 minutes)

- Teacher (or confident pupil) plays 'Ode to Joy' with both hands on the piano while the pupils follow the score. What are the six elements of music contained in this piece? (Rhythm, pitch, texture, tempo, dynamics and structure.)

Main – Composing using six elements of music (45 minutes)

- Pupils continue the composing project on page 10 of their workbooks. Using 'Ode to Joy' as a model, the piece should have the following (the first three were already discussed last lesson):
    - RHYTHM: melody uses crotchets, dotted crotchets, quavers and minims
    - PITCH: melody uses the notes CDEFG; mainly stepwise; recognisable shape
    - STRUCTURE: four four-bar phrases in 4/4 time; A clear phrase structure that has both repetition and contrast
    - TEXTURE: notes in the left hand using the notes CDEFG and crotchets, dotted crotchets, quavers and minims providing a variety of texture (monophonic, heterophonic, polyphonic, homophonic)
    - DYNAMICS: markings such as p, f and cresc.
    - TEMPO: markings such as Allegro and rit.

Plenary – Perfoming composition on the keyboard (10 minutes)

- Some pupils play their work-in-progress to the rest of the class (if they prefer, the teacher can play it). Does their piece have all the features listed above?

Lesson 7 – Instruments

Objectives

- All pupils differentiate between broad types of instrument (wind, strings, percussion, other)
- Many pupils identify more specific families: bowed/plucked strings, woodwind/brass, pitched/unpitched percussion, keyboard/pop & jazz
- Some pupils identify specific instruments and voice types: violin, electric guitar, flute, trumpet, xylophone, etc.

Resources

- Pupils' workbooks
- 5 packs of instrument cards – each pack has 32 cards with the name and picture of an instrument
- Musical Instrument audio examples:
  http://www.musictechteacher.com/music_learning_theory/music_instruments.htm

Procedure

Starter: instruments - appraising (10 minutes)

- The teacher divides the whiteboard into 8 equal sections, labelled as follows:

STRINGS	WIND	PERCUSSION	OTHER
Plucked	Woodwind	Pitched	Keyboard
Bowed	Brass	Unpitched	Pop & Jazz

- Pupils suggest instruments which the teacher writes into the relevant box.
- Pupils complete the table on page 9 of their workbooks.

Main: instruments – appraising/listening (20 minutes)

- The teacher rubs out the instruments (but not the section headings) and divides the pupils into groups of 3-4 – they sit on the carpet. The teacher gives a pack of instrument cards to each group.
- The groups must work together to divide the instrument cards equally amongst the 8 'families' of instruments, in the same layout as on the whiteboard. Which group can divide them up first?
- Led by the teacher, the class discusses the differences between the instruments within each family, particularly in relation to PITCH (e.g. the violin is the highest and the double bass is the lowest bowed string instrument).
- The teacher plays Musical Instrument audio examples from the weblink.

Plenary – Composing using all seven elements of music (30 minutes)

- Pupils continue the composing project on page 10 of their workbooks. In addition to the six elements of music listed in the last lesson, the pupils should now choose an instrument for the beginning of the piece and another instrument from a different family later in the piece.

Lesson 8 - Conclusion

Objectives

- To demonstrate knowledge of families and instruments
- To finish composing a piece which demonstrates all seven elements of music

Resources

- Pupils' workbooks
- 5 packs of instrument cards – each pack has 32 cards with the name and picture of an instrument
- Musical Instrument Quiz: https://www.youtube.com/watch?v=d4S3yXtAC9Y

Procedure

Starter: Musical Instrument Quiz - listening (10 minutes)

- Pupils turn to page 12 of their workbooks
- The teacher plays the Musical Instrument Quiz (also showing the video, so that the numbers of the questions are clear)
- In the table on page 12 of their workbooks., the pupils write their 20 answers to the Music Instrument Quiz
- The exercise is marked out of 40 - half a mark if Family is not specific (i.e. strings/wind/percussion/other); half a mark if instrument itself is not spelled correctly

Number	Family	Instrument
1	Other (½) / Pop & Jazz (1)	Saxophone
2	Other (½) / Keyboard (1)	Piano
3	Wind (½) / Woodwind (1)	Flute
4	Other (½) / Keyboard (1)	Harpsichord
5	Strings (½) / Bowed Strings (1)	Cello
6	Wind (½) / Brass (1)	Tuba
7	Strings (½) / Bowed Strings (1)	Viola
8	Percussion (½) / Unpitched percussion (1)	Cymbal
9	Percussion (½) / Unpitched percussion (1)	Triangle
10	Wind (½) / Brass (1)	French Horn
11	Other (½) / Keyboard (1)	Organ
12	Strings (½) / Plucked Strings (1)	Guitar
13	Wind (½) / Brass (1)	Trumpet
14	Strings (½) / Bowed Strings (1)	Violin
15	Wind (½) / Brass (1)	Trombone
16	Wind (½) / Woodwind (1)	Oboe
17	Strings (½) / Plucked Strings (1)	Harp
18	Wind (½) / Woodwind (1)	Bassoon
19	Strings (½) / Bowed Strings (1)	Double Bass
20	Wind (½) / Woodwind (1)	Flute

Main: Composing (40 minutes)

- Pupils complete their keyboard compositions demonstrating all seven elements of music.

Plenary: Performing compositions (10 minutes)

- Some pupils perform their composition to the rest of the class; other compositions are played by the teacher

Extra Activity: Musical Happy Families

An optional extra activity using the instrument cards

- The teacher divides the pupils into groups of 3-4 – they sit on the carpet. The teacher gives a pack of instrument cards to each group.
- The teacher explains the rules of the Musical Happy Families card game:
    - One pupil in each group is chosen to be the dealer. The dealer shuffles and deals the cards.
    - The pupils pick up their cards but MUST NOT show the other pupils.
    - The dealer is the first pupil to ask ONE other pupil in the group, do you have the [instrument] from the [family], e.g. 'Do you have the harp from the plucked string family?'
    - If the other pupil DOES have the card, they hand it to the first pupil, who then has another turn.
    - If the other pupil DOES NOT have the card, it is their turn.
    - When a pupil has a whole family of four cards, they place the four cards face-up in front of them.
    - The person with the most families when all the cards are used up OR when the teacher stops the game is the winner within that group.

Families of instruments as categorised in the card game

A. Bowed strings
   1. Violin
   2. Viola
   3. Cello
   4. Double Bass

B. Plucked strings
   1. Acoustic Guitar
   2. Harp
   3. Ukulele
   4. Banjo

C. Woodwind
   1. Flute
   2. Oboe
   3. Clarinet
   4. Bassoon

D. Brass
   1. French Horn
   2. Trumpet
   3. Trombone
   4. Tuba

E. Pitched percussion
   1. Xylophone
   2. Glockenspiel
   3. Tubular Bells
   4. Timpani

F. Unpitched percussion
   1. Bass drum
   2. Snare Drum
   3. Tom toms
   4. Cymbal

G. Keyboards
   1. Piano
   2. Harpsichord
   3. Organ
   4. Celesta

H. Pop & Jazz
   1. Electric Guitar
   2. Bass Guitar
   3. Synthesiser
   4. Saxophone

Xylophone	Glockenspiel	Tubular bells	Timpani
Bass drum	Snare drum	Tom toms	Cymbal
Piano	Harpsichord	Organ	Celesta
Electric Guitar	Bass Guitar	Synthesiser	Saxophone

Picture credits

All pictures either public domain or reproduced under the Creative Commons Licence

Cover – OpenClipArtVectors https://pixabay.com/p-159870/?no_redirect

Violin – Pianoplonkers https://upload.wikimedia.org/wikipedia/commons/f/f4/German,_maple_Violin.JPG

Viola – Just plain Bill https://upload.wikimedia.org/wikipedia/commons/c/cd/Bratsche.jpg

Cello - Georg Feitscher https://en.wikipedia.org/wiki/Cello#/media/File:Cello_front_side.png

Double Bass – Ian Burt https://www.flickr.com/photos/oddsock/208182066

Guitar – Martin Möller https://en.wikipedia.org/wiki/Guitar#/media/File:GuitareClassique5.png

Harp – Martin Kraft https://commons.wikimedia.org/wiki/File:Harp_Illustration.svg

Ukulele – Arent https://commons.wikimedia.org/wiki/File:Ukulele1.jpg#/media/File:Ukulele1.jpg

Banjo – Dmacks https://en.wikipedia.org/wiki/Banjo#/media/File:BluegrassBanjo.jpg

Flute - ClkerFreeVectorImages https://pixabay.com/en/flute-music-classic-jazz-play-306396/

Oboe - ClkerFreeVectorImages https://pixabay.com/p-34796

Clarinet - ClkerFreeVectorImages https://pixabay.com/p-31372

Bassoon – Celtic_Minstrel https://en.wikipedia.org/wiki/File:BassoonRotated.jpg

French Horn – Fluteflute https://en.wikipedia.org/wiki/French_horn#/media/File:French_horn_front.png

Trumpet – PJ https://commons.wikimedia.org/wiki/File:Trumpet_1.png

Trombone - ClkerFreeVectorImages https://pixabay.com/en/trombone-brass-musician-mouthpiece-25688/

Tuba -   Open Clip Art Library https://commons.wikimedia.org/wiki/File:Tuba_01.svg

Xylophone - ClkerFreeVectorImages https://pixabay.com/en/xylophone-sticcado-instrument-music-308025/

Glockenspiel - flamurai https://commons.wikimedia.org/wiki/File:Glockenspiel-malletech.jpg

Tubular Bells – Xylosmygame https://simple.wikipedia.org/wiki/Tubular_bells#/media/File:Deagan_chimes.jpg

Timpani – vxla https://commons.wikimedia.org/wiki/File:Lefima_Timpani.jpg

Bass drum – Open Clip Art Library https://commons.wikimedia.org/wiki/File:Bass_drum.svg

Snare Drum – Vladimir Morozov https://commons.wikimedia.org/wiki/File:Snare_drum_-_Vladimir_Morozov.jpg

Tom toms – ZooFari https://en.wikipedia.org/wiki/Tom-tom_drum#/media/File:TomTom.JPG

Cymbal - Stephan Czuratis https://en.wikipedia.org/wiki/Cymbal#/media/File:2006-07-06_Crash_Zildjian_14.jpg

Piano – Steinway & Sons https://commons.wikimedia.org/wiki/File:Steinway_%26_Sons_concert_grand_piano,_model_D-274,_manufactured_at_Steinway%27s_factory_in_Hamburg,_Germany.png

Harpsichord – FREYmanagement https://en.wikipedia.org/wiki/List_of_period_instruments#/media/File:Harpsichord_VitalJulianFrey.jpg

Organ – Joe Mabel https://commons.wikimedia.org/wiki/File:Wesleyan_University_-_Memorial_Chapel_organ_05.jpg

Celesta – Museumsinsulaner https://commons.wikimedia.org/wiki/File:Celesta_Schiedmayer_MIM_1592.jpg

Electric Guitar – Spike78 https://commons.wikimedia.org/wiki/File:Electric_Guitar_(Superstrat_based_on_ESP_KH_-_vertical)_-_with_hint_lines_and_numbers.png#/media/File:Electric_Guitar_(Superstrat_based_on_ESP_KH_-_vertical).png

Bass Guitar – Itsthatemo https://en.wikipedia.org/wiki/Bass_guitar#/media/File:Stingray_guitar.jpg

Synthesiser – Torley https://commons.wikimedia.org/wiki/File:Roland_V-Synth.png

Saxophone - ↄ https://commons.wikimedia.org/wiki/File:Saxophone_alto2.png

Hands on keyboard – author's photo

Rock 'n' Roll

KS3 Scheme of Work – 6 lessons

Objectives

- To learn about the origins of rock 'n' roll in the 1950s
- To sing and play several rock 'n' roll and rock songs
- To recognise some typical instruments – keyboard, drums and double bass – and their functions
- To play the chords of C, F, G and Am on the keyboard
- To perform the 12-bar blues and I-vi-IV-V chord progressions on the keyboard
- To arrange a rock 'n' roll song for a group performance

Lesson Overview

1. The Origins of Rock 'n' Roll
2. The 12-Bar Blues
3. The Bass Line
4. The I-vi-IV-V Progression
5. Preparing Group Arrangement
6. Group Performances and Listening Exercise

Subject-specific vocabulary

- Performers: Bill Haley and the Comets, Elvis Presley
- Instruments: double bass, drum kit, keyboard
- Chords: C, F, G, Am
- 12-bar blues and I-vi-IV-V chord progressions

Assessments

- Performing (keyboard) – 12-bar blues
- Composing – group arrangement of a Rock 'n' Roll song
- Listening – Hound Dog

This topic can be followed up with the topic on The Beatles, which introduces more secondary triads and more complex song structures, reflecting the development of rock music in the 1960s.

Lesson 1: The Origins of Rock 'n' Roll

Resources

- Pupil's worksheet: 'Origins of Rock 'n' Roll'
- YouTube video of 'Rock Around the Clock': https://www.youtube.com/watch?v=ZgdufzXvjqw
- Lyrics for 'Rock Around the Clock': http://www.oldielyrics.com/lyrics/bill_haley_and_the_comets/rock_around_the_clock.html
- YouTube video on the History of Rock 'n' Roll: https://www.youtube.com/watch?v=R-j2rILarYA
- Drum kit, including bass drum, snare drum and hi-hat
- Portable classroom percussion instruments resembling bass drum, snare drum and hi-hat

Procedure

Starter – Performing (singing)

- Listen to/watch YouTube video of 'Rock Around the Clock' as pupils come into class
- From lyrics on board, learn to sing, 'Rock Around the Clock', phrase by phrase
- Perform the song as a class
- Quick oral questions: What style of song is this? (Rock 'n' Roll.) Which decade? (1950s.)

Main - Listening

- Watch YouTube video on the History of Rock 'n' Roll and answer questions on worksheet
- Watch teacher's demonstration of the different instruments on the drum kit and label diagram on worksheet
- Watch teacher's demonstration of a basic rock rhythm on the drum kit:
    - Closed hi-hat plays on all four beats of each bar (more advanced – two quavers per beat)
    - Bass drum plays on 1st and 3rd beats of each bar
    - Snare drum plays on 2nd and 4th beats of each bar

Plenary – Performing (percussion)

- Pupils practise this rhythm as body percussion

    - Right hand crossed over left hand plays 'hi-hat' on left thigh (left-handers play left hand on left thigh, without crossing over)

    - Right foot taps 'bass drum' on floor, keeping the heel on the ground

    - Left hand crossed under right hand plays 'snare drum' on right thigh (left-handers play right hand on right thigh, without crossing over)

- Some pupils take turns performing the basic rock rhythm on the drum kit

Lesson 2: The 12-Bar Blues

Resources

- Worksheets on 'The 12-bar blues'
- YouTube video of Elvis Presley singing 'Blue Suede Shoes':
    - https://www.youtube.com/watch?v=T1Ond-OwgU8
- Lyrics of Blue Suede Shoes: http://www.azlyrics.com/lyrics/elvispresley/bluesuedeshoes.html

Procedure

Starter: Performing (singing)

- Listen to and watch YouTube video of Elvis Presley singing 'Blue Suede Shoes' as pupils come into class
- Learn to sing, phrase by phrase, 'Blue Suede Shoes' from lyrics
- Perform the song as a class

Main: Listening

- Work out how many bars long the repeating chord sequence is by listening to the teacher play the first verse of 'Blue Suede Shoes' and calling out the numbers in the lyrics: 1, 2, 3.
- Continue this sequence until you reach the end of the verse. (Remember there are four beats in each bar.) How many bars long is the chord sequence? (12 bars).
- Watch teacher demonstrating the chords C, F and G on a keyboard.
- Write a dot on the THREE notes in each chord on the worksheet (the first one is done for you).
- Notate the chords C, F and G and write the notes in each chord on the worksheet.
- Listen to your teacher playing the 12-bar blues and write down the chord sequence. There should be one chord (C, F or G) in each box. Chords can be repeated. Remember there are four beats in every bar.

Main: Performing (keyboard)

- Go to keyboards in pairs (more able keyboard/piano players go by themselves); bring worksheets
- Practise playing the chords C, F and G as a class (out loud, without headphones)
- If you find playing the whole chord difficult, just play the first note of each chord
- Practise playing the 12-bar blues chord sequence as a class (out loud, without headphones)
- Practise playing the 12-bar blues chord sequence with headphones. The task can be differentiated as follows:
    - Less able pupils play the bass line (root of each chord) on the left hand side
    - More able pupils play the chords on the right hand side
    - Most able pupils play bass line in the left hand and chords in the right hand

Plenary: Performing (keyboard)

- Some pupils play work-in-progress to rest of class

Lesson 3: The Bass Line

Resources

- Double bass or, if not available, YouTube video
  https://www.youtube.com/watch?v=cNiMc9n38oI
- Worksheet on 'The Bass Line'
- Worksheets on 'The 12-bar blues' and 'The 12-bar blues – fully notated version'
- Keyboards and headphones

Procedure

Starter: Listening

- Pupils listen to teacher (or YouTube video) demonstrating the double bass
- Pupils read through work

Main: Performing (keyboard)

- One or two pupils demonstrate the 12-bar blues chord progression (RH chords only with root-only bass line in the LH)
- Teacher now demonstrates walking bass line on extension worksheet for more able pupils
- Pupils continue practising the 12-bar blues chord sequence with headphones, now with a walking bass line if possible. The task can be differentiated as follows:
    - Less able pupils play the root-only bass line on the left hand side
    - More able pupils play the walking bass on the left hand side or chords on the right hand side
    - Most able pupils play walking or root-only bass line in the left hand and chords in the right hand

Plenary: Performing (keyboard)

- Pupils perform 12-bar blues on the keyboard to the rest of the class
- The performance is assessed by teacher using the following criteria:
    - Plays root of each chord (as bass line or part of chord)
    - Plays three note chord (together or broken)
    - Maintains steady pulse
    - Plays syncopated rhythm and/or walking bass
    - Plays with both hands together

Lesson 4: The I-vi-IV-V Progression

Objectives

- To recognise the I-vi-IV-V progression in a variety of songs
- To learn to play the I-vi-IV-V progression on the keyboard

Resources

- Worksheet on 'The I-vi-IV-V Progression'
- YouTube video clip of 'Heart and Soul': https://www.youtube.com/watch?v=YsIL07eOqOU

Procedure

Starter: Performing/Listening

- Teacher invites a pair of pupils to play 'that' duet on the piano/keyboard. (There are probably two pupils who can play the very familiar piano duet 'Heart and Soul', although they may well not know its title.)
- Pupils watch the YouTube video clip of 'Heart and Soul' from 1938 to see the origin of this song and to hear the chord progression that is used.

Main: Appraising

- Pupils read the introduction to 'The I-vi-IV-V progression' and the many songs it has been used for
- Pupils complete the chord diagrams for F and G

Main: Performing (keyboard)

- In pairs, pupils prepare their own duet arrangement of the I-vi-IV-V progression in whatever style they choose. This could be the familiar 'Heart and Soul' arrangement, or perhaps in the style of one of the other songs on the list.

Plenary: Performing (keyboard)

- Pupils perform their duet arrangements of the I-vi-IV-V progression to the rest of the class.

Lesson 5: Preparing Group Arrangement

Resources

- Worksheets from previous lessons on 'The 12-bar blues' and 'The I-vi-IV-V progression'
- Lyric sheets depending on chosen songs (printed during the lesson)
- Practice rooms/breakout areas with keyboards
- Drum kit and similar unpitched percussion instruments

Procedure

Starter – Listening

- Teacher explains that the pupils have a lesson and a half to prepare a group performance of a rock 'n' roll song using either the 12-bar blues or the I-vi-IV-V progressions
- Each group is made up of 3-6 pupils as follows:
    - 2 pupils (or 1 more able pupil) singing the melody
    - 2 pupils (or 1 more able pupil) playing bass and chords on the keyboard
    - 2 pupils (or 1 more able pupil) playing the drum kit or similar unpitched percussion instruments
- The pupils (or teacher) should print out the required lyrics from the internet

Main – Performing (singing, keyboard and percussion)

- The groups go to practice rooms and other breakout areas to practise, monitored by the teacher.

Plenary - (singing, keyboard and percussion)

The small groups perform their work-in-progress to the rest of the class. (The teacher can start the composing/arranging assessment.)

Lesson 6: Group performances and listening exercise

Resources

- Worksheets from previous lessons on 'The 12-bar blues' and 'The I-vi-IV-V progression'
- Lyric sheets depending on chosen songs (printed during the lesson)
- Practice rooms/breakout areas with keyboards
- Drum kit and similar unpitched percussion instruments
- 'Listening to Rock 'n' Roll' (unseen listening exercise)
- YouTube audio clip of 'Hound Dog': https://www.youtube.com/watch?v=-eHJ12Vhpyc

Procedure

Starter – Performing (singing, keyboard and percussion)

- Groups practise their Rock 'n' Roll songs for the last time

Main – Performing (singing, keyboard and percussion)

- The groups perform their arrangement of the Rock 'n' Roll song to the rest of the class.
- The teacher completes the composing/arranging assessment.

Plenary - Listening

- Teacher distributes 'Listening to Rock 'n' Roll' (unseen listening exercise)
- Pupils complete the listening exercise on Rock 'n' Roll, which brings together concepts learnt throughout the topic, including the 12-bar blues, instrumentation, chords, and structure

Extension/cover work

The musical *Grease!* is set in an American high school in 1959 and contains songs in a rock 'n' roll style, as well as portraying American teenage life in the 1950s. The 1978 film version starring John Travolta and Olivia Newton-John is not entirely appropriate for children, but the 2016 *Grease Live* is usable. The following YouTube clips from *Grease Live* demonstrate different songs which can be performed by pupils using either the 12-bar blues or I-vi-IV-V chord progressions:

12-bar blues

- 'Greased Lightning'
  https://www.youtube.com/watch?v=ZBzFq3M291U&index=2&list=RD_pnL1quIayA

I-vi-IV-V progression

- 'Those Magic Changes'
  https://www.youtube.com/watch?v=_pnL1quIayA&list=RD_pnL1quIayA#t=105
- 'Rock 'n' Roll is Here to Stay' https://www.youtube.com/watch?v=d1QgI-q4LRA
- 'We Go Together' https://www.youtube.com/watch?v=AqAwtTk7HUQ

The lyrics can be found at https://lyrics.az/soundtracks/grease-live/

Listening to Rock 'n' Roll

Hound Dog

1. Who is singing this song? Tick the correct box. [1]
   - ☐ Bill Haley
   - ☐ Elvis Presley
   - ☐ The Beatles
   - ☐ Bruno Mars

2. What decade is this song from? Tick the correct box. [1]
   - ☐ 1930s
   - ☐ 1940s
   - ☐ 1950s
   - ☐ 1960s

3. What is the name of the chord progression that is used? .... [1]

4. Fill in the THREE missing chords in the chord progression below. [3]

C	C		C
F		C	C
	F	C	C

5. Which instrument is playing the chords? .... [1]

6. Which instrument is playing the bass line? .... [1]

7. Which collection of unpitched percussion instruments is playing a rhythm? .... [1]

8. Which one of these unpitched percussion instruments plays a ROLL (very quickly repeated notes) at the end of each verse? .... [1]

TOTAL [10 marks]

37

Listening to Rock 'n' Roll **ANSWERS**

Hound Dog

1. Who is singing this song? Tick the correct box. [1]
   - ☐ Bill Haley
   - ✓ Elvis Presley
   - ☐ The Beatles
   - ☐ Bruno Mars

2. What decade is this song from? Tick the correct box. [1]
   - ☐ 1930s
   - ☐ 1940s
   - ✓ 1950s
   - ☐ 1960s

3. What is the name of the chord progression that is used? 12-BAR BLUES [1]

4. Fill in the THREE missing chords in this chord progression. [3]

C	C	<u>C</u>	C
F	<u>F</u>	C	C
<u>G</u>	F	C	C

5. Which instrument is playing the chords? ELECTRIC GUITAR (½ mark for GUITAR).. [1]

6. Which instrument is playing the bass line? DOUBLE/STRING BASS (½ mark for BASS) [1]

7. Which collection of unpitched percussion instruments is playing a rhythm? DRUM KIT/SET (½ mark for DRUMS) [1]

8. Which one of these unpitched percussion instruments plays a ROLL (very quickly repeated notes) at the end of each verse? SNARE/SIDE DRUM .... [1]

TOTAL [10 marks]

Rock 'n' Roll: Assessment Sheet

CLASS ___ Name	Performing *12-Bar Blues on keyboard*					Composing *Rock 'n' Roll song for small group*					Listening *Hound Dog*					Comments
	Plays first note of each chord (bass line)	Plays three note chord (together or	Maintains steady pulse	Syncopated rhythm and/or walking bass	Hands together	Maintains sense of pulse	Rhythmic variety in part	Listens to others in group	Plays different pitches (or percussion)	Performs with confidence and style	Identifies context of Rock n Roll (qus	Identifies chord progression and key (qus	Identifies chords in progression (qu 4)	Identifies string instruments (qus 5, 6)	Identifies percussion instruments (qus 7,	

39

The Beatles

KS3 Scheme of Work – 6 lessons

Objectives

- To understand how to form primary and secondary triads in C major on the keyboard
- To learn, through listening and performing, common chord sequences using these triads
- To arrange a Beatles song for a group performance

Lesson Overview

7. Love Me Do
8. Eleanor Rigby
9. Let it Be
10. Can't Buy Me Love
11. Arranging a Beatles song
12. Performing a Beatles song

Subject-specific vocabulary

- Tonality: major and minor
- Chords: C, F, G, Dm, Em, Am
- Chord sequences: I-V-vi-IV, circle progression
- Timbres and textures: electric guitar, bass guitar, drum kit

Assessments

- Performing (keyboard) – 'Love Me Do' (Lesson 1)
- Listening – 'Can't Buy Me Love' (Lesson 3)
- Composing – arrangement of a Beatles song for group performance (Lesson 6)

Lesson 1: Love Me Do

Objective
- To learn about instrumentation, song structure and primary triads
- To perform a chord sequence using C, F and G major chords

Resources
- YouTube video clip of Love Me Do: https://www.youtube.com/watch?v=Jbt8oH5Lxto
- Pupils' worksheets:
    - 'Meet The Beatles/Electric and Bass Guitars'
    - 'Love Me Do'
- Electric and bass guitars for demonstration (if possible)
- Keyboards and headphones

Procedure

Starter: Appraising
- Who were the Beatles and what instruments did they play?
- Demonstration and comparison of electric guitar and bass guitar (electric bass)
- The bass guitar is different from the electric guitar because there are 4, not 6, strings which play lower than the electric guitar. The four strings are tuned the same as the first four strings of the guitar: to E, A, D and G

Main: Listening
- Listen to the Beatles singing 'Love Me Do'
- Note how C feels like the 'home chord' in the key of C major; F and G are different; G pulls back to C
- Fill in the chords on the worksheet 'Love Me Do' using the clues given
- Note structural features: intro, verse with refrain, middle eight, final repeated chorus to fade

INTRO	VERSE	CHORUS	VERSE	CHORUS	MIDDLE EIGHT	VERSE	CHORUS	MIDDLE EIGHT	VERSE	CHORUS

- Discuss the instruments you hear in the song (two electric guitars – lead and rhythm, bass guitar, drum kit and harmonica)
- Additional questions which can be asked orally:
    - Which instrument is playing the solo during the intro? HARMONICA or MOUTH ORGAN [played by John Lennon]
    - Which previous section is the chorus based on? INTRO (in fact, in the original version, John Lennon plays the harmonica solo in counterpoint to Paul McCartney singing the chorus/refrain)
    - The middle eight is used twice in this song – can you spot the difference between the two sections? THE FIRST TIME IS VOCAL AND THE SECOND TIME IS INSTRUMENTAL

Plenary: Performing

- Pupils practise perform 'Love Me Do' on the keyboard. Most pupils work in pairs, playing bass line or chords with one hand (if there is one of each at one keyboard, the bass line should be on the left-hand side)
- Teacher guides pupils and completes the performing assessment, over more than one observation if necessary, as different skills are seen:
    - Plays roots of different chords on the keyboard (this could be single notes forming a bass line, or part of a triad, or three-note chord)
    - Forms different triads on keyboard (this can just be C and F in the verse/chorus)
    - Plays correct chord sequence (assessment of one section of the song is sufficient, in order to save time)
    - Plays with sense of pulse (either on every beat or playing a rhythm that fits in with the four beats in a bar)
    - Plays bass in left hand and chords in right hand (more able pupils playing hands together)
- If there is time, some pupils are chosen to demonstrate to the rest of the class

Lesson 2: Eleanor Rigby

Objectives

- To hear the difference between major and minor chords
- To learn how to form the chords Dm, Em and Am on the keyboard
- To play a Beatles song using one major and one minor chord

Resources

- Pupils' worksheets:
    - 'Major and Minor Chords'
    - 'Eleanor Rigby'
- YouTube clip of Eleanor Rigby: https://youtu.be/HuS5NuXRb5Y
- Keyboards and headphones

Procedure

Starter: Listening

- Teacher plays several major and minor triads in different keys, in a random order. The pupils say whether they think the chord is major or minor. Keep going until all the pupils are confident in telling the difference

Main: Listening

- Pupils try out triads (three-note chords) on the white notes of the keyboard, using the same shape as the ones they have learnt: C, F and G. What do they notice about most of the other triads? (The triads based on D, E and A are all minor.) Extension question: is there a triad which is neither major nor minor? (Yes – B diminished.)
- Fill in the chord diagrams and notes for Dm, Em and Am on the worksheet 'Major and Minor Chords'
- Work out the number of semitones between the notes in major and minor triads
- Now listen to the original recording of 'Eleanor Rigby' by the Beatles, completing the chord sequence and song structure on the worksheet 'Eleanor Rigby':

INTRO	VERSE 1	CHORUS	VERSE 2	CHORUS	MIDDLE 8 = INTRO	VERSE 3	CHORUS + INTRO

- Additional questions:
    - What is unusual about the accompanying instruments? They form a string group (double string quartet).
    - Which section is heard again after the second chorus, in the place of a middle eight? The intro.
    - Which two sections are combined at the end of the piece? The chorus and the (melody of) the intro.

Plenary: Performing

- Go back to the keyboards and play through the chord sequence of 'Eleanor Rigby':
    - Firstly, slowly, without playing along to the Beatles' recording
    - Then, faster, playing along to the Beatles' recording

Lesson 3: Can't Buy Me Love

Objectives

- To use the full range of primary triads (I, IV, V) and secondary triads (ii, iii, vi) in a Beatles song
- To learn how to use the 'circle progression', where the root of a chord rises by a fourth

Resources

- YouTube clip of the Beatles' song 'Can't Buy Me Love': https://youtu.be/srwxJUXPHvE
- Lyrics for 'Can't Buy Me Love': https://www.azlyrics.com/lyrics/beatles/cantbuymelove.html
- Pupils' worksheets:
    a. 'Can't Buy Me Love'
    b. 'Listening Exercise: The Beatles'
- Practice rooms with digital pianos
- Drum kit and similar unpitched percussion instruments

Procedure

Starter – Listening/Performing

- Pupils listen to the Beatles' song 'Can't Buy Me Love'
- Pupils learn to sing 'Can't Buy Me Love'

Main – Appraising

- Pupils complete the chord sequence for 'Can't Buy Me Love' using the clues given, under the teacher's guidance

Plenary - Listening

- Pupils complete the worksheet 'Listening Exercise: The Beatles'

Teacher assesses listening exercise using the mark scheme below:

1. (Each VERSE/CHORUS in the correct place scores half a mark, up to a maximum of 3 marks)

| INTRO | VERSE | VERSE | CHORUS | VERSE | SOLO | CHORUS | VERSE | OUTRO |

2. Up to three instruments in any order:
    - Electric/lead/rhythm guitar [one mark] (only half a mark for 'guitar') – award two marks for 'electric guitar' and 'rhythm guitar' if listed separately
    - Bass guitar or electric bass [one mark] (only one mark for 'bass')
    - Drum kit or drum set [one mark] (only half a mark for 'drums')
3. 12-bar blues [two marks] (only one mark for '12-bar' or 'blues')
4. Bar 11 [one mark] (it is F instead of C)
5. Bar 3 – C [one mark] / Bar 6 – F [one mark]
6. Primary/major triads [two marks] (only one mark for 'triads' or 'major' or 'primary']
7. Secondary/minor triads [two marks] (only one mark for 'triads' or 'minor' or 'secondary']
8. No marks for liking or disliking the song. One mark for naming a musical element: pitch, duration, tempo, timbre, texture, dynamics or structure; another mark for describing the musical element appropriately (high/low, long/short, fast/slow, etc.)

Lesson 4: Let it Be

Objectives
- To learn to play a song using the common I-V-vi-IV chord sequence
- Sadfasdf

Resources
- Pupils' worksheets on 'Let it Be'
- Vimeo clip of the Beatles' 'Let it Be': https://vimeo.com/79815584 [it is difficult to find the original version of 'Let it Be' on YouTube, presumably for copyright reasons]
- Keyboards and Headphones

Procedure

Starter – Listening
- Listen to the Beatles' original version of 'Let it Be'

Main – listening
- Listen to the song once or twice more, completing the chord sequence and song structure on the worksheet 'Let it Be':

INTRO	VERSE 1	CHORUS	VERSE 2	CHORUS	MIDDLE EIGHT	CHORUS	VERSE 3	CHORUS

- Additional questions which can be asked orally:
    - Which instrument is playing the intro? Piano [played by Paul McCartney]
    - What additional sound comes into the song at the beginning of the second verse? Backing vocals/choir
    - What additional sound comes into the song at the beginning of the first chorus? Drum kit [played by Ringo Starr]
    - Which earlier bars of which section are bars 1-4 of the middle eight based on? The last two bars of the verse or chorus (bars 7-8 of the verse or bars 3-4 of the chorus); they are repeated.
    - Which new instrument is introduced in bars 3-4 of the middle eight? (Hammond) organ [played by Billy Preston]
    - Which section are bars 5-8 of the middle eight based on? The verse.
    - Which new instrument is introduced in bars 5-8 of the middle eight? Electric guitar [played by George Harrison]

Plenary – Performing (keyboard)
- Learn to play the chord sequence for 'Let it Be' on keyboards

Lesson 5: Arranging a Beatles song

Objectives
- To arrange a Beatles song for a group of pupils playing different instruments

Resources
- Song sheets from previous lessons on 'Love Me Do', 'Eleanor Rigby' and 'Let it Be'
- Practice rooms with digital pianos
- Drum kit and similar unpitched percussion instruments
- Pupils' worksheets:
    a. Love Me Do
    b. Eleanor Rigby
    c. Can't Buy Me Love
    d. Let it Be

Procedure

Starter - arranging
- Teacher explains that the pupils will begin to arrange and practise one of the four Beatles songs as a group.
- Teacher assigns the following Beatles songs to four mixed ability groups:
    - Love Me Do
    - Eleanor Rigby
    - Can't Buy Me Love
    - Let it Be

Main – arranging
- Each group is made up of 3-6 pupils as follows:
    - 2 pupils (or 1 more able pupil) singing the melody
    - 2 pupils (or 1 more able pupil) playing bass and chords on the keyboard
    - 2 pupils (or 1 more able pupil) playing the drum kit or similar unpitched percussion instruments
- The groups go to practice rooms and other breakout areas to practise, monitored by the teacher

Plenary - performing
The small groups perform their work-in-progress to the rest of the class

The teacher can start the composing/arranging assessment

Lesson 6: Performing a Beatles song

Objectives
- To perform a Beatles song for a group of pupils playing different instruments

Resources
- Song sheets from previous lessons on 'Love Me Do', 'Eleanor Rigby' and 'Let it Be'
- Practice rooms with digital pianos
- Drum kit and similar unpitched percussion instruments
- 'Can't Buy Me Love' listening exercise

Procedure

Starter – Appraising
- Teacher goes over assessment criteria for group arrangement (see below)

Main – Performing (singing, keyboard and percussion)
- Groups practise their Beatles songs
- Each group is made up of 3-6 pupils as follows:
    - 2 pupils (or 1 more able pupil) singing the melody
    - 2 pupils (or 1 more able pupil) playing bass and chords on the keyboard
    - 2 pupils (or 1 more able pupil) playing the drum kit or similar unpitched percussion instruments

Plenary - Performing
- Pupils perform their group Beatles song arrangements to the rest of the class
- Teacher assesses performances according to the following criteria:
    - Maintains sense of pulse
    - Rhythmic variety in part
    - Listens to others in group
    - Plays different pitches (or percussion)
    - Performs with confidence and style

The Beatles: Assessment Sheet

CLASS ___ Name	Performing — *Love Me Do* (keyboard): Plays roots of different chords / Forms different triads (three-note chords) / Plays correct chord sequence / Plays with sense of pulse / Plays bass in left hand and chords in right	Listening — *Can't Buy Me Love*: Identifies verse/chorus within structure (qu 1) / Identifies instruments in rock band (qu 2) / Identifies chords in song (qus 3–5) / Completes notation of melody (qu 6) / Expresses/justifies opinion about song (qu 7)	Arranging — Beatles song for small ensemble: Maintains sense of pulse / Rhythmic variety in part / Listens to others in group / Plays different pitches (or percussion) / Performs with confidence and style	Comments

Baroque Music

KS3 scheme of work – 6-8 lessons

Objectives

- To listen to music from the Baroque Era (1600-1750) in a variety of genres by several composers
- To perform part of Pachelbel's *Canon* on the keyboard
- To compose a melody above the ground bass of Pachelbel's *Canon*

Lesson overview

- Lesson 1: Pachelbel's *Canon*
- Lesson 2: Scarlatti's *Sonata*
- Lesson 3: Bach's *Toccata and Fugue*
- Lesson 4: Handel's *Messiah*
- Lesson 5: Purcell's *Dido and Aeneas*
- Lesson 6: Vivaldi's *Four Seasons*
- Lesson 7/8: Group composition and performance

N.B. The last two lessons are optional and can be completed in one lesson if necessary.

Vocabulary

- Genres
    - Sonata – piece for solo instrument(s) in several movements
    - Oratorio - religious story in several movements with singers and orchestra (not staged)
    - Opera - non-religious story in several movements with singers and orchestra (staged)
    - Concerto – piece for soloist(s) and orchestra in several movements
- Movements within vocal works
    - Chorus – where the choir sings
    - Aria – a solo song
    - Recitative – a style of story-telling, halfway between normal speech and singing
    - Overture – a scene-setting piece for the orchestra (without singing)
- Ground bass (ostinato)
- Bass clef and bass stave notation
- Instruments:
    - Bowed string family (violin, viola, cello, double bass)
    - Keyboard instruments (harpsichord and organ)

Assessment

- Performing: part of Pachelbel's *Canon* on the keyboard
- Composing: a melody above the ground bass of Pachelbel's *Canon*
- Listening: short exercises on different genres of Baroque music

Lesson 1 - Pachelbel's *Canon*

Objectives

1. To compare three different versions of Pachelbel's *Canon*
2. To identify the string instruments in a piece of Baroque Music
3. To play the bass line for Pachelbel's *Canon* from letter and/or staff notation

Resources

- YouTube clips of Pachelbel's *Canon* in different styles:
  - Pachelbel's Canon in D w/ hip hop https://www.youtube.com/watch?v=oex4S3vPKR4
  - J. Pachelbel. Canon in D Major https://www.youtube.com/watch?v=PfxrNblTr4o
  - CANON IN D - by Paulinho Winterle http://www.youtube.com/watch?v=kN61_VrTzRU
  - Pupils' worksheets – 'Listening to Pachelbel's Canon' and 'Pachelbel's Canon – sheet music'
- Keyboards

Procedure

Starter – Listening

- Listen to three different versions of a piece of music (about 1½ minutes of each) and answer the following questions orally:
  - Which do you think is the original version? (2nd VERSION.) Why? (IT DOES NOT USE MODERN INSTRUMENTS/STUDIO TECHNIQUES.)
  - Which family do all the instruments belong to (see below)? (STRINGS.) What are they? (VIOLIN, VIOLA, CELLO, DOUBLE BASS, HARPSICHORD.)
  - Can you notice any repeating patterns in the music? (YES – IN THE BASS LINE)

Main – Listening

- Pupils label the instruments on the worksheet 'Listening to Pachelbel's Canon'.
- Listen to the original (second) version of Pachelbel's Canon again and answer the questions at the bottom of the worksheet 'Listening to Pachelbel's Canon':
1. Which instrument begins the piece? CELLO
2. What is the name of the repeating pattern it plays? OSTINATO/GROUND BASS
3. The second and third instruments to play are the 1st and 2nd VIOLINS
4. What is the fourth instrument to play? VIOLA
5. Which instrument is playing chords (more than one note at the same time)? HARPSICHORD

Main – Performing

- Learn to play the bass line for Pachelbel's *Canon* using only the thumb and fourth finger of the left hand from letter notation. (Most pupils can share a keyboard in pairs and play the ground bass at different octaves in pairs.)
- EXT: start learning hands together from 'Pachelbel's Canon - sheet music' – one to a keyboard

Plenary – Performing

- One or two pupils play the bass line Pachelbel's *Canon* to class
- One or two pupils play the melody and the bass line hands together
- The teacher explains that all pupils will be learning the melody, either hands separately or hands together

Lesson 2 - Scarlatti's Sonata

Objectives
- To listen to a Baroque keyboard sonata
- To play the bass line, and possibly the melody, for Pachelbel's *Canon* on the keyboard

Resources
- YouTube link for Scarlatti's Sonata http://www.youtube.com/watch?v=6a92bOaJxBo
- Pupils' worksheets 'Scarlatti's Sonata', 'Listening to Pachelbel's Canon' and 'Pachelbel's Canon – sheet music'
- Keyboards

Procedure

Starter - listening
- Listen to Scarlatti's Sonata and answer the questions on the worksheet:
    1. What instrument is this played on? HARPSCHORD
    2. What is the tempo of the music? 'ANDANTE COMMODO' – AT A STEADY WALKING PACE
    3. How many beats are there in a bar? 3 (3 CROTCHETS IN A BAR)
    4. Is the piece in a major or minor key? MAJOR (E MAJOR)
    5. How does the ⁀ symbol affect the notes? DECORATES OR ORNAMENTS THEM (MORDENT)

Main - performing
- Continue to practise playing Pachelbel's *Canon* on the keyboard, reading from notation.
- Many pupils will have acquired this skill and can now start learning the right hand melody hands separately. They can continue to work in pairs on the keyboard, with the pupil on the left hand side playing the ground bass. If that pupil is also ready to learn the melody, the pupils can swap around halfway through the practising time.
- Pupils who can play hands together progress as far as they can with the three lines of melody with the bass line. (The third is the most challenging, as it consists of two melody notes per bass note.)

Plenary - performing
- Some pupils play their work-in-progress on Pachelbel's *Canon* to class – teacher completes ongoing Performing assessment

Lesson 3 - Bach's Toccata and Fugue

Objectives

- To listen to an organ piece by Bach
- To learn how to work out intervals from letter-names
- To work out the intervals between the bass and melody at the beginning of Pachelbel's Canon

Resources

- YouTube link of Bach's Toccata and Fugue http://www.youtube.com/watch?v=F4JQZb83oCc
- Pupils' worksheets 'Scarlatti's Sonata', 'Listening to Pachelbel's Canon' and 'Pachelbel's Canon – sheet music'
- Keyboards

Procedure

Starter - Listening

- Listen to the beginning of Bach's Toccata and Fugue and answer questions
    1. Look at the picture of Bach the instrument he composed this piece for. What is this instrument? ORGAN
    2. Look at the music below. Why are there three staves, not two, as for harpsichord or piano music? TWO STAVES FOR THE MANUALS (HANDS) AND ONE STAVE FOR THE PEDALS (FEET)
    3. How does the tempo change in the first section of the piece? IT GETS FASTER
    4. Is the piece in a major or minor key? MINOR
    5. What word would you use to describe the mood of the piece? DRAMATIC/CREEPY/SPOOKY/SCARY (OR SIMILAR)

Main - performing

- Continue to practise playing Pachelbel's *Canon* on the keyboard, reading from notation.
- Many pupils will have acquired this skill and can now start learning the right hand melody hands separately. They can continue to work in pairs on the keyboard, with the pupil on the left hand side playing the ground bass. If that pupil is also ready to learn the melody, the pupils can swap around halfway through the practising time.
- Pupils who can play hands together progress as far as they can with the three lines of melody with the bass line. (The third is the most challenging, as it consists of two melody notes per bass note.)

Plenary - performing

- All pupils play Pachelbel's *Canon* to the class – teacher completes final Performing assessment

Lesson 4 – Handel's Messiah

Objectives
- to listen to a sequence of short movements from Handel's *Messiah*, and analyse what type of movement each one is
- to compose a melody above Pachelbel's ground bass using notes from the underlying chords

Resources
- YouTube clips from Handel's *Messiah*:
    - Pastoral Symphony https://youtu.be/mpqmgdISWzM
    - 'There were shepherds… Glory to God' https://www.youtube.com/watch?v=kVB5r-ui-C8
    - 'Rejoice greatly, o daughter of Zion' https://www.youtube.com/watch?v=z1xlYIoekE8
- Pupils' worksheets:
    - 'Handel's Messiah'
    - 'Pachelbel's Canon – sheet music'
    - 'Performing and Composing using Pachelbel's Canon'
- Keyboards

Procedure

Starter - listening
- Read through the worksheet 'Handel's Messiah'. Learn what an oratorio is, and the different type of movements to expect within it: chorus, aria, recitative and overture
- Listen to the sequence from Handel's *Messiah* and answer questions:
  1. Handel's Messiah is an example of an ORATORIO.
  2. 'Pastoral Symphony' is a type of OVERTURE.
  3. 'There were shepherds abiding in the field' is an example of RECITATIVE.
  4. 'Glory to God in the highest' is an example of a CHORUS.
  5. 'Rejoice greatly, o daughter of Zion' is an example of an ARIA.

Main – composing
- Read through the explanation of 'Composing using the ground bass' on the worksheet 'Performing and Composing using Pachelbel's Canon'
- Taking turns in pairs at the keyboards, pupils compose their own 4-bar melody on the blank stave above the fifth line of the ground bass. Each note of the melody should be a minim (two-beat note) taken from the underlying chord and the melody should not jump around too much.
- (EXT) More able pupils compose another 4-bar tune to a repetition of the ground bass. They can also use passing and/or auxiliary notes – non-chord notes that are a step away from chord notes and progress to a chord note straight away.

Plenary - performing
- Some pupils play their work-in-progress to class, accompanied by their partner playing the ground bass, OR the teacher plays both hands.

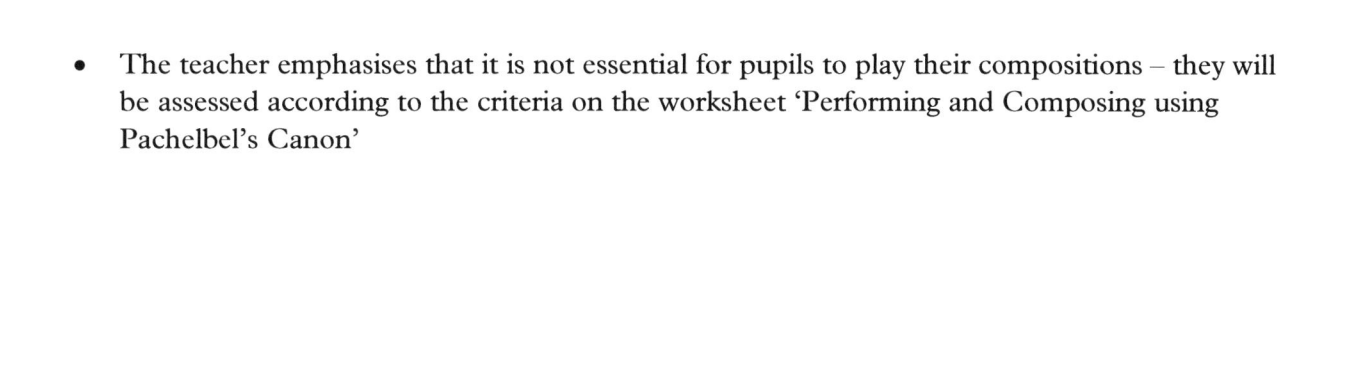

- The teacher emphasises that it is not essential for pupils to play their compositions – they will be assessed according to the criteria on the worksheet 'Performing and Composing using Pachelbel's Canon'

Lesson 5 - Purcell's Dido and Aeneas

Objectives
- To listen to part of a Baroque opera in English
- To perform Pachelbel's Canon with own composition

Resources
- YouTube clip of the last scene of 'Dido and Aeneas': https://youtu.be/6GmJdPYC2Xw?t=44m33s (starting at 44 minutes, 33 seconds)
- Pupils' worksheets:
    - 'Purcell's Dido and Aeneas'
    - 'Pachelbel's Canon – sheet music'
    - 'Performing and Composing using Pachelbel's Canon'

Procedure

Starter – appraising/listenhing
- Pupils read through the worksheet 'Purcell's Dido and Aeneas'
- Listen to the last scene of 'Dido and Aeneas' (it is not essential to listen to the whole chorus) and answer the questions about final scene:
    1. What is the style of the section starting 'Thy hand, Belinda'? RECITATIVE
    2. What kind of bass line is used in Dido's aria 'When I am laid in earth'? REPEATING/OSTINATO/GROUND BASS
    3. What kind of key is Dido's aria in? MINOR
    4. What type of movement follows Dido's aria? CHORUS
    5. What family of instruments accompanies the opera? STRINGS

Main – composing
- Taking turns in pairs at the keyboards, pupils continue to compose their own 8-bar melody on the blank staves above the fifth and sixth lines of the ground bass. Each note of the melody should be a minim (two-beat note) taken from the underlying chord and the melody should not jump around too much.
- (EXT) More able pupils use passing and/or auxiliary notes – non-chord notes that are a step away from chord notes and progress to a chord note straight away.

Plenary - performing
- Some pupils play their work-in-progress to class, accompanied by their partner playing the ground bass, OR the teacher plays both hands.
- The teacher emphasises that it is not essential for pupils to play their compositions – they will be assessed according to the criteria on the worksheet 'Performing and Composing using Pachelbel's Canon'

Lesson 6 - Vivaldi's Four Seasons

Objectives

- To listen to 'Spring' from Vivaldi's *Four Seasons*
- To complete composition based on Pachelbel's *Canon*

Resources

- YouTube clip of 'Spring' from Vivaldi's *Four Seasons*: https://www.youtube.com/watch?v=aFHPRi0ZeXE
- Pupils' worksheets:
    - 'Vivaldi's Four Seasons'
    - 'Pachelbel's Canon – sheet music'
    - 'Performing and Composing using Pachelbel's Canon'
- Keyboards

Procedure

Starter – listening

- Pupils read through the worksheet 'Vivaldi's Four Seasons' and answer the questions:
  1. Describe the tempo of this movement. FAST (ALLEGRO)
  2. What family of instruments is used in this concerto? STRINGS
  3. What is the solo instrument? VIOLIN
  4. Do the dynamics change suddenly or gradually? SUDDENLY
  5. Fill in the table below with the pitch, rhythm, dynamics and articulation for each section:

high	low	low-high	high
quick	slow	quick	quick
soft	soft	loud	soft
detached	smooth	detached	detached

Main – composing

- Taking turns in pairs at the keyboards, pupils complete their 8-bar their own 4-bar melody on the blank staves above the fifth and sixth lines of the ground bass. Each note of the melody should be a minim (two-beat note) taken from the underlying chord and the melody should not jump around too much.
- (EXT) More able pupils use passing and/or auxiliary notes – non-chord notes that are a step away from chord notes and progress to a chord note straight away.

Plenary - performing

- Some pupils play their work-in-progress to class, accompanied by their partner playing the ground bass, OR the teacher plays both hands.
- The teacher assesses the composition according to the Assessment Sheet

Lessons 7/8: Group composition and performance

Objective
- to form an instrumental group to compose and perform a piece inspired by Baroque music.

Resources
- Pupils' worksheets:
    - 'Group composition and performance'
    - 'Pachelbel's Canon – sheet music'
    - 'Vivaldi's Four Seasons'
    - 'Handel's Water Music'
- Classroom instruments and pupils' own instruments for group performance
- Recording equipment

Procedure

Starter – composing
- Teacher explains that the pupils have one or two lessons to form an instrumental group to compose and perform a piece inspired by Baroque music
- Pupils read through the worksheet 'Group composition and performance' and choose one of the following options:
    - Pachelbel's *Canon*
    - Vivaldi's *Four Seasons*
    - Handel's *Water Music*

Main – composing/performing
- Pupils practise their group compositions/performances in practice rooms or breakout areas
- Teacher goes around the groups, advising as required

Plenary – composing/performing
- Pupils perform their work-in-progress (first week) or final piece (second week)
- In the final week, the teacher optionally records the piece and the pupils listen to it

Baroque Music: Assessment Sheet

CLASS __ / Name	Performing — Pachelbel Canon					Composing — Pachelbel Canon					Listening — Baroque Music						Comments
	Correct pitches in left hand (ground)	Correct pitches in right hand (melody)	Correct fingering	Hands together	Sense of flow/legato	Legible, clear music notation	All notes taken from underlying chord	Good melodic shape	Mainly conjunct	Passing/auxiliary notes	Pachelbel Canon	Scarlatti Sonata	Bach Toccata and Fugue	Handel Messiah	Purcell Dido and Aeneas	Vivaldi Four Seasons	

African Music

KS3 scheme of work
N.B. This is designed as a modular scheme of work with self-contained lessons linked by recurring themes. It works well in a short half of term and/or one interrupted by trips, exams, etc. Lessons 3 and 4 work best when taught consecutively.

Objectives

- Performing: to sing traditional African songs and to play African percussion
- Composing: to create a layered, syncopated rhythmic ostinato within a group performance
- Listening: to learn about, and to recognise, African musical styles and instruments

Lesson overview

- Lesson 1: Wimmoweh
- Lesson 2: African instruments
- Lesson 3: African rhythms
- Lesson 4: Group composition
- Lesson 5: Singing African Songs
- Lesson 6: Listening to African Music
- Research assignment (cover lesson/homework – no listening required)

Vocabulary

- African instruments:
    - CABASA large gourd with a handle covered with a network of stringed beads
    - KORA a harp with 21 strings, resounding in half a large gourd, covered with skin
    - TALKING DRUM A drum with two heads which are kept taut by strings
    - MARIMBA A set of wooden bars arranged in a row over a set of resonating gourds
    - DJEMBE A large single-headed drum
    - THUMB-PIANO A wooden board with thin metal strips attached to it
- Polyrhythm and cross rhythm
- Call-and-response
- Ostinato
- Layering
- A capella
- Close and parallel harmony

Assessment

- Performing: singing an African song (Lesson 5)
- Composing: creating a rhythmic ostinato as part of a group composition/performance (Lessons 3 and 4)
- Listening: 'Listening to African Music' (Lesson 6)

Lesson 1: Wimmoweh

N.B. This lesson can be made shorter by just singing the melody of the song, or singing it with a simple (not chordal) ostinato.

Objective

- To gain a practical understanding of some typical features of African music by singing the traditional Zulu song 'Wimmoweh'
- To apply the understanding to three unfamiliar pieces of African music

Resources

- YouTube link of 'Wimmoweh' ('The Lion Sleeps Tonight') https://www.youtube.com/watch?v=hPXrdoWyGc0
- Pupil's Worksheet 'African Music'
- YouTube clips:
    1. Brekete music from Ghana https://www.youtube.com/watch?v=AX6XK7WbsLY
    2. Ladysmith Black Mambazo - Abezizwe ngeke bayiqede https://www.youtube.com/watch?v=rc9hqvo4qhU
    3. The Drummers of Burundi https://www.youtube.com/watch?v=iecVcVsmrnY

Procedure

Starter: Listening

- Listen to and watch Timon and Pumbaa's version of 'Wimmoweh' ('The Lion Sleeps Tonight') thinking about the following questions:
    - Which continent does this song come from? (Africa.)
    - Is there another sung part apart from the main tune? (Yes – sung to 'Wimmoweh.)
    - What do you notice about this other part? (Repeated/ostinato.)

Main: Performing

- Learn to sing the melody of 'Wimmoweh' ('The Lion Sleeps Tonight') by ear. Repeat each line after the teacher (call-and-response)★
- Learn to sing the I-IV-I-V 'Wimmoweh' ostinato (in C major: C-F-C-G)
- The class splits into 3 equal groups; each group sings the ostinato for a given verse while the other two groups sing the melody
- The ostinato can optionally be enhanced by close parallel harmony (one of the groups singing the third, as opposed to the root, of each chord)
- This class performance can optionally be accompanied by African drums playing the beat/rhythmic ostinato and/or keyboard(s) playing the I-IV-I-V bass/chord ostinato

Plenary: Listening

- Discuss these features of 'Wimmoweh' which are typical of African music: cross-rhythms, parallel harmony, a capella, percussion, voices, close harmony, call-and-response
- Listen to 3 pieces of African music and answer questions on them (Pupil's Worksheet 'Listening to African Music')

* The copyright lyrics are available from numerous websites, for example
http://www.lyricsfreak.com/l/laurie+berkner/wimoweh+the+lion+sleeps+tonight_20808527.html

Lesson 2: African instruments

Objective

- To learn about some traditional African instruments and how they are played
- To apply this knowledge to recognising some traditional African instruments in a listening exercise

Resources

- YouTube video of 'Traditional African Music Instruments'
  https://www.youtube.com/watch?v=ejMLRrKY9IU
- Pupil's worksheets: 'African Instruments (1)' and 'African Instruments (2)'
- YouTube audio links
    1. **Mbira** Tinashé: Mbira version of "Zambezi"
       https://www.youtube.com/watch?v=fb9qoEHLgVo
    2. **Kora** Toumani Diabaté & Ballaké Sissoko 1999 Récital duo de kora YouTube
       https://www.youtube.com/watch?v=hnTDuahaXwg
    3. **Balafon** Balafon style Sénoufo - Adama Diabaté - Niangoya
       https://www.youtube.com/watch?v=kXXhp_bZvck
    4. **Shekere** Yosvany Terry Shekere Solos
       https://www.youtube.com/watch?v=mmJm91UPGfs
    5. **Talking drum** Talking Drummer from Nigeria
       https://www.youtube.com/watch?v=wkAF_7IItFY

Procedure

Starter: Listening

- Pupils watch YouTube video of Traditional African instruments and see how many they can remember
- Pupils recall as many instruments as they can:
    - Kalimba (or thumb piano)
    - Algaita (wind instrument from West Africa)
    - Mbira (another thumb piano from East and Southern Africa)
    - Balafon (a pitched percussion instrument with wooden keys and resonating gourds)
    - Kora (a harp strung over a large resonating gourd)
    - Shekere (a cabasa with beads strung over a resonating gourd)
    - Djembe (a single-headed hand drum from Central and West Africa)
    - Udu (a drum like a ceramic pot)
    - (bamboo pipes shown but not labelled)
    - Talking drum (double headed drum with adjustable heads)
    - Marimba (a type of xylophone)
- Discuss how many African instruments are made from natural or found materials, like gourds

Main: Appraising

- Identify 6 instruments from pictures (qu1)
- Answer questions on the instruments (qu2)

Plenary: Listening

- Identify and describe the five instruments by listening to them (qu3).

Lesson 3: African Rhythms

Objective
- To listen to rhythmic ostinati and to represent them using grid notation
- To compose own syncopated rhythm using grid notation

Resources
- Recording of African musician introducing percussion instruments in a layered piece: https://clyp.it/gkg2n1sl
- Pupil's worksheet on 'African Rhythms'
- Unpitched percussion instrument (preferably African) for each pupil

Procedure

Starter (listening)
- Listen to recording of African musician introducing percussion instruments in a layered piece (without referring to workbook)
- Which instruments can you remember?
    - Cowbells
    - Cabasa
    - Kome drum
    - Kagano drum
    - Kiri drum
    - Congas
    - Sogo
    - Talking drum
- Is there anything else you notice about the music? (Syncopation, ostinati, cross rhythms etc.)

Main (listening/performing/composing)
- Discuss the grid notation on page 41 and practise clapping on the beat, twice every beat, and off the beat
- As a class, clap the different instruments' rhythms on page 41, without then with the recording
- Complete the missing rhythm for the Kome drum
- Compose own rhythm on single line using blank grid notation – try to include syncopation
- Practise counting and clapping to help composing
- When each pupil's rhythm is completed, they can choose an unpitched percussion instrument
- Practise playing own rhythm on unpitched percussion instrument

Plenary (composing)
- Each pupil plays their rhythm in front of the class
- Assessed by the teacher by giving a mark for the first three of the five composing criteria for this topic:
    - Notates a rhythm using grid notation
    - Composes a rhythm with syncopation
    - Plays a rhythm in time with pulse

Lesson 4: Group composition

N.B. This lesson follows on from Lesson 3: African rhythms, which should be completed before Lesson 4 is attempted.

Objective

- To develop rhythm composed last lesson so it forms part of a layered group composition
- To perform unpitched percussion as a group in front of the class

Resources

- Music Workbook page 41 ('African Rhythms')
- Unpitched percussion instrument (preferably African) for each pupil
- Blank grid notation on whiteboard (either drawn or projected on slide)

Procedure

Starter (performing/listening)

- Teacher selects three or four more able pupils who are confident about performing in front of the class; they each select the same unpitched percussion instrument as last lesson
- On the blank grid notation on the whiteboard, each pupil notates their own rhythm on a blank row
- Each pupil performs their rhythm on their percussion instrument as an ostinato
- The teacher brings in another 'layer' (i.e. a new ostinato) one at a time and stops the group together
- Teacher explains that this is an example of the group composition/performance that all pupils are working on in this lesson
- Teacher explains that each pupil must try to keep their own ostinato going and start/finish at different times to create a layered texture

Main (composing/performing)

- The class splits into groups of 3, 4 or 5
- Each pupil copies the rhythms from the other pupils in their group into their own grid notation
- Each pupil selects the same unpitched percussion instrument as last lesson
- The groups practise their group composition/performance in different spaces, monitored by the teacher
- Pupils must co-operate as a group, keep their own ostinato going and decide how to start/finish at different times to create a layered texture

Plenary (composing/performing/listening)

- Groups perform their group composition to the rest of the class
- Teacher assesses the remaining two composing criteria for each pupil:
    - Maintains a different ostinato from group
    - Starts or stops as an independent layer

Lesson 5: Singing African Songs

Objective
- To widen experience of singing African songs to include South African protest songs
- To demonstrate ability to sing solo in front of the class

Resources
- Pupil's worksheet 'Two South African Protest Songs'
- Audio clip of 'The Children of Africa' http://www.songsforteaching.com/folk/asikatali-childrenofafrica.php
- Audio clip of 'Siyahamba' http://ingeb.org/spiritua/siyahamb.html

Procedure

Starter (performing)
- Sing through 'Wimmoweh' (learnt in Lesson 1)

Main (performing)
- Learn to sing 'The Children of Africa' and 'Siyahamba'
- Discuss the purposes and contexts of these songs (protest songs)
- Teacher explains about the years of apartheid (racial division) in South Africa)

Plenary (performing)
- Each pupil sings the first verse from their choice of the three songs to the rest of the class
- Teacher marks the performance on assessment grid according to the following criteria:
    - Sings one verse in front of class
    - Sings with good tuning
    - Sings with good sense of rhythm
    - Sings with a well-supported voice
    - Sings with clear diction

Lesson 6: Listening to African Music

Objectives

- To widen experience of listening to African Music to include popular music
- To consolidate understanding throughout the topic in a listening exercise

Resources

- Recordings of three African pop songs
- Worksheets on 'African pop music' and 'Listening to African Music'
- Recordings for 'African pop music':
  - *Mo Bero Agba* by King Sunny Adé and his African Beats https://www.youtube.com/watch?v=EtaAMSyql4I
  - *Hluphekile* by Soul Brothers https://www.youtube.com/watch?v=tNKwKtY7Rgc
  - *Mosese 2000* by Somo Somo https://soundcloud.com/sterns-music/mosese-2000-edit-poleni-edit
- Recording for 'Listening to African Music':
  - Africa Forestdance perform Sosisa https://www.youtube.com/watch?v=BkaBGwfekis

Procedure

Starter (listening)

- Listen to the three examples of African pop music without workbook
  - *Mo Bero Agba* by King Sunny Adé and his African Beats
  - *Hluphekile* by Soul Brothers
  - *Mosese 2000* by Somo Somo
- Discuss how this compares to the pop music that pupils usually listen to

Main (listening)

- Read about the three pieces already listened to
- Listen to the pieces again, and, using the printed information together with what the music sounds like, fill in the 'African' and 'Pop' influences for each piece

Plenary (listening)

- Pupils complete 'Listening to African Music' worksheet
- Marked by the teacher out of 15 (see next page for answers)
- the responses are summarised on the assessment sheet as follows:
  - Recognises a plucked string instrument (qus 1-3)
  - Recognises a pitched percussion instrument (qus 4-6)
  - Recognises a shaken percussion instrument (qus 7-9)
  - Recognises a struck percussion instrument (qus 10-12)
  - Identifies other musical features (qus 13-15)

Listening to African Music: answers

Africa Forestdance perform Sosisa

1st instrument to be played

1. What is this instrument?   KORA .... [1]
2. What family does it belong to?   STRINGS .... [1]
3. How is it played?   PLUCKED .... [1]

2nd instrument to be played

4. What is this instrument?   BALAFON .... [1]
5. What family does it belong to?   PITCHED PERCUSSION .... [1]
6. How is it played?   HIT WITH BEATERS .... [1]

3rd instrument to be played

7. What is this instrument?   SHEKERE .... [1]
8. What family does it belong to?   UNPITCHED PERCUSSION .... [1]
9. How is it played?   SHAKEN .... [1]

4th instrument to be played

10. What is this instrument?   DJEMBE or CONGAS.. [1]
11. What family does it belong to?   UNPITCHED PERCUSSION .... [1]
12. How is it played?   HIT WITH HANDS .... [1]

Other musical features

13. What is the name of the repeating pattern that the instruments play?   OSTINATO .... [1]
14. What word describes the texture, where the instruments play one at a time?   LAYERED .... [1]
15. What word describes the off-beat rhythms that the instruments play?   SYNCOPATION .... [1]

African Music: assessment sheet

CLASS __	Performing *Singing*	Composing *Group drumming*	Listening *African Music*	Comments
Name	Sings one verse in front of class / Sings with good tuning / Sings with good sense of rhythm / Sings with a well-supported voice / Sings with clear diction	Notates a rhythm using grid notation / Composes a rhythm with syncopation / Plays a rhythm in time with pulse / Maintains a different ostinato from group / Starts or stops as an independent layer	Recognises a plucked string instrument / Recognises pitched percussion (qus 4-6) / Recognises shaken percussion (qus 7-9) / Recognises an African drum (qus 10-12) / Identifies other musical features (qus 13-15)	

72

Year 8

Film Music
Caribbean Music
Indian Music
Classical Music
Jazz

Film Music

KS3 Scheme of Work (6-8 lessons)

Objectives

- To become familiar with music for different films and to recognise film genres
- To learn how some musical features can be combined to create soundtracks for different film genres
- To perform a film music theme on the keyboard, and to adapt it to compose for a film clip

Overview

- Lesson 1: Film and Genre
- Lesson 2: Musical Ideas for Film Genres
- Lesson 3*: Orchestral Film Music
- Lesson 4: Listening to the James Bond Theme
- Lesson 5: Practising the James Bond Theme
- Lesson 6: Performing the James Bond Theme
- Lesson 7*: Composing film music
- Lesson 8*: Final evaluation of composition
- Cover lesson/homework worksheets:
    - Sound effects for film
    - Creative sound effects
    - A Century of Film Music (2 pages)

* Lessons 3, 7 and 8 are self-contained lessons which can be omitted for a shorter scheme of work

Subject-specific vocabulary

- Film genres: thriller, romance, cartoon, comedy, sci-fi, western
- Musical features: cluster chords, 'oom-pah' accompaniment, atonal, major, minor, chromatic
- Timbres: synthesiser, strings, brass

Assessments

- Performing (keyboard) – The James Bond Theme
- Listening – Film Genres, James Bond Theme with score and in context of a film
- Composing – Goldfinger pre-credits sequence

Lesson 1 – Film and Genre

Objective
- To assess the suitability of music for film
- To discuss and identify different film genres

Resources
- YouTube videos of three film clips: first version with switched soundtracks, second with correct soundtracks
    - 1st playing https://youtu.be/o0-OLpoK_v8
    - correct soundtracks https://youtu.be/XN44Hts--Xk
- Pupils' worksheets:
    - 'Matching Music to Film'
    - 'Film and Genre'

Procedure

Starter – Listening
- Watch video clip of 3 film clips. (They have switched soundtracks, but pupils should not be aware of this.)
- Discuss the suitability of each film with each soundtrack
- Suggest how the clips could be swapped for better effect
- Watch 3 film clips with correct soundtracks – discuss whether it is an improvement

Main – Appraising
- Pupils read the introduction on worksheet 'Film and Genre'.
- Discuss the characteristics of each genre as a class.
- Which genre would you say each of the films 1-3 on the previous page belong to?
- Give an example of a film and its genre.

Plenary - Listening
- Pupils listen to ten excerpts of film music (1-10) and decide which genre each one belongs to: Thriller, Sci-Fi, Western or Cartoon.
- On 'Matching Music to Film' worksheet, pupils are going to listen to ten short extracts taken from different soundtracks of films and identify what film genre they think best matches the extract choosing from – Thriller, Sci-Fi, Western or Cartoon.
- Answers below:
    1. Western (The Good, the Bad and the Ugly)
    2. Sci-Fi (Bladerunner/Alien?)
    3. Thriller (Goldfinger)
    4. Cartoon (The Flintstones)
    5. Western (The Magnificent Seven)
    6. Thriller (Schindler's List?)
    7. Cartoon (Popeye)
    8. Sci-Fi
    9. Thriller (Indiana Jones)
    10. Sci-Fi

Lesson 2 – Musical Ideas for Film Genres

Resources

- YouTube video 'Movies & Music in the Park 2014 "Seasons and Genres"': https://www.youtube.com/watch?v=sbmk7XLk6oE
- Pupils' worksheet 'Musical Ideas for Film Genres'
- Small pieces of paper labelled A-J, cut out and folded, enough for one per keyboard

Procedure

Starter – Listening

- Watch YouTube video 'Movies & Music in the Park 2014 "Seasons and Genres"' (0.00-0.40). How many film genres can you spot? Watch again and see if you can name the genres.
- What are the characteristics of the music for these film genres? Here are some possible answers:-
  - Western – sweeping, upbeat symphony
  - orchestra
  - Cartoon – fast, 'oom-pah' accompaniment with brass and/or plucked strings
  - Sci-fi – atonal/whole tone melodies played on synthesisers and other unusual timbres
  - Thriller – rhythmic, chromatic, minor key

Main – Composing

- The teacher gives the pupils (in pairs or individually on the keyboard) a 'musical idea' (A-J)
- Pupils go in pairs on keyboards, with more able pupils working by themselves
- Using the musical ideas, pupils compose a short (20-30 second) piece of music for your genre.

Plenary – Performing

- Pupils play their interpretation of the musical idea to the rest of the class, who listen and answer the following questions:
  - Which musical idea (A-J) did they play?
  - Which film genre does each musical idea suit best?
- Pupils write TWO musical ideas for each film genre in the table.

Lesson 3 – Orchestral Film Music

Objective
- To consolidate and develop knowledge of orchestral instruments
- To listen to and analyse orchestral music used in films

Resources
- Pupils' worksheets 'The Symphony Orchestra' and 'Orchestral Film Music'
- YouTube clips of orchestral excerpts:
    A. Joplin: Rag Time Dance https://www.youtube.com/watch?v=unGmMmD8kPQ
    B. Bartók: Music for Strings, Percussion, and Celesta (3rd movt.)
       https://www.youtube.com/watch?v=3bro-ofOxVM
    C. Mozart: Clarinet Concerto (2nd movt.)
       https://www.youtube.com/watch?v=BxgmorK61YQ
    D. R. Strauss: Also Sprach Zarasthustra (opening)
       https://www.youtube.com/watch?v=jbDVk8fwor0
    E. Wagner: Ride of the Valkyries (orchestral version)
       https://www.youtube.com/watch?v=YriqxxKkNfQ

Procedure

Starter – Appraising
- Pupils read the introduction on the worksheet 'The Symphony Orchestra' and look at the diagram of the orchestra
- Pupils fill out the table on the worksheet 'The Symphony Orchestra', listing the instruments in each family, from highest pitch to lowest pitch

Main - Listening
- Pupils read the description of Films 1-5 and write down the genre of each film
- Pupils listen to excerpts A-E and match them to the films
- Pupils Listen to excerpts A-E again and write notes on why they think this music is appropriate for the genre. They might mention elements such as instruments, tempo, dynamics, and tonality (major, minor, or atonal).

Plenary - Appraising
- Teacher goes over answers with the class

Lesson 4 – Listening to the James Bond Theme

Objectives
- to listen to the James Bond theme, identifying layers of the texture
- to work out the notes of the bass pedal, chromatic riff and electric guitar riff

Resources
- James Bond theme – YouTube link: https://www.youtube.com/watch?v=Ii1tc493bZM
- Pupils' worksheet: 'The James Bond Theme'
- Keyboards and headphones
- James Bond sheet music http://www.007museum.com/James%20Bond%20-%20dr%20No.pdf

Procedure

Starter - Listening
- Listen to film music clip. What series of films does it come from? (James Bond.)

Main – Listening
- Pupils listen again to the James Bond theme, answering questions on worksheet 'The James Bond Theme'
  1. Is the music in a major or a minor key? MINOR (E)
  2. What do you notice about the bass line? IT REPEATS/STAYS THE SAME (PEDAL)
  3. The riff around middle C is chromatic. What does this mean? MOVES BY SEMITONES
  4. How many different notes (pitches) does the electric guitar riff use? THREE (E, F#, G)
- Pupils fill in the grid with the letter-names of the notes, using the given clues and trying out the riffs on a keyboard.

Plenary - Appraising
- The class go over the answers, filling in a grid on the board with the help of the teacher
- All pupils make sure they have the correct answers on their own grid, because they will start practising the James Bond theme in the next lesson

Lesson 5 – Practising the James Bond Theme

Objective

- To practise one or more of the James Bond themes on the keyboard, according to ability

Resources

- Pupils' worksheet: 'The James Bond Theme' (with grid completed during last lesson)
- James Bond sheet music http://www.007museum.com/James%20Bond%20-%20dr%20No.pdf
- Keyboards and headphones

Procedure

Starter - Appraising

- Teacher introduces the performing task and goes through the assessment criteria, demonstrating how each of the 15 points can be fulfilled

Main – Performing (keyboards)

- Each pupil chooses a tune to start learning depending on their ability on the keyboard. Here are the tasks in order from the least to the most challenging:
  1. The bass ostinato, in either the simpler or harder version (both are on the beat so not syncopated; the simpler version is a pattern of three chromatic notes going up and down, the harder version is the same, but alternating with pedal note)
  2. The electric guitar riff, most of which uses three notes (E, F#, G) but is rhythmically syncopated and challenging
  3. The trumpet tune, which leaps around a lot, uses chromatic notes and is rhythmically syncopated and challenging
  4. The bass ostinato in the left hand at the same time as the other tune(s) in the right hand.
- As far as possible, each pupil playing the bass ostinato (1) should go in a pair with another pupil playing the electric guitar riff (2) or the trumpet tune (3). Any pupils who are confident playing the bass ostinato with one of the other tunes (4) should go by themselves.
- All pupils should start with the bass ostinato, then some progress onto the electric guitar riff and a few to the trumpet tune. (They should play as many as possible in order to achieve the best mark of which they are capable.)
- Practise playing the tunes together, guided by teacher.

Plenary – Performing (keyboards)

- Some pupils perform their work-in-progress to the rest of the class
- Pupils can take their worksheets home to practise and read through the assessment criteria

Lesson 6 – Performing the James Bond Theme

Objective
- To perform one or more of the James Bond themes on the keyboard, according to ability

Resources
- Pupils' worksheet: 'The James Bond Theme' (with grid completed with letter-names)
- James Bond sheet music http://www.007museum.com/James%20Bond%20-%20dr%20No.pdf
- Keyboards and headphones

Procedure

Starter - Appraising
- Teacher explains that the performances will be assessed at the end of this lesson
- Teacher reminds pupils briefly the assessment criteria, demonstrating how each of the 15 points can be fulfilled

Main – Performing (keyboards)
- Each pupil chooses a tune to start learning depending on their ability on the keyboard. Here are the tasks in order from the least to the most challenging:
    1. The bass ostinato, in either the simpler or harder version (both are on the beat so not syncopated; the simpler version is a pattern of three chromatic notes going up and down, the harder version is the same, but alternating with pedal note)
    2. The electric guitar riff, most of which uses three notes (E, F#, G) but is rhythmically syncopated and challenging
    3. The trumpet tune, which leaps around a lot, uses chromatic notes and is rhythmically syncopated and challenging
    4. The bass ostinato in the left hand at the same time as the other tune(s) in the right hand.
- As far as possible, each pupil playing the bass ostinato (1) should go in a pair with another pupil playing the electric guitar riff (2) or the trumpet tune (3). Any pupils who are confident playing the bass ostinato with one of the other tunes (4) should go by themselves.
- All pupils should start with the bass ostinato, then some progress onto the electric guitar riff and a few to the trumpet tune. (They should play as many as possible in order to achieve the best mark of which they are capable.)
- Practise playing the tunes together, guided by teacher

Plenary – Performing (keyboards)
- All pupils perform to the rest of the class, assessed by the teacher

Lesson 7 – Composing Film Music

Objectives

- To identify ways in which themes and sound effects are used in a film clip
- To compose music for a film clip using pre-existing themes, new themes and sound effects

Resources

- Pupils' worksheets:
    - 'James Bond – Incidental Music'
    - 'Composing Incidental Music'
- YouTube clips of the pre-title sequence of *Goldfinger*
    - James Bond Goldfinger Clip https://youtu.be/q_gkOA-rcK0
    - James Bond Goldfinger clip 2nd half only https://youtu.be/KZypBQC84HE
- James Bond sheet music http://www.007museum.com/James%20Bond%20-%20dr%20No.pdf
- Keyboards and headphones
- Various composing methods as available:
    - music notation or sequencer software
    - blank, lined or manuscript paper
    - classroom instruments and pupils' own instruments

Procedure

Starter - Listening

- Watch short clip from beginning (pre-title sequence) of *Goldfinger*
- Pupils write the letter for each music cue opposite the visual cues in the film
- Teacher goes through answers with class:

1.	Spy shoots through gun barrel	C
2.	Guards patrolling factory	J
3.	Camera moves from factory to lake	K
4.	Duck moves towards lake's edge	I
5.	James Bond comes out of the water	F
6.	Guard is knocked out by James Bond	G
7.	Guard disappears behind cooling tower	A
8.	James Bond goes inside cooling tower	D
9.	James Bond applies plastic explosive	E
10.	CUT to interior of bar	H
11.	CLOSE UP of wristwatch reaching zero	B

Main – Composing

- Pupils watch the second half of the pre-title sequence of *Goldfinger* (which does not have any music)
- Pupils complete the visual cue sheet (left hand column)
- Pupils note preliminary music ideas (right hand column)
- Each pupil can now choose their preferred method of composition from those available in the classroom
- Pupils try out preliminary musical ideas on instruments/computers

Plenary – Performing

- Some pupils perform their work in progress, either on their instrument or on the computer

Lesson 8 – Final evaluation

Objectives
- To complete composition using pre-existing themes, new themes and sound effects

Resources
- Pupils' worksheets:
    - 'James Bond – Incidental Music'
    - 'Composing Incidental Music'
- YouTube clips of the pre-title sequence of *Goldfinger*
    - James Bond Goldfinger Clip https://youtu.be/q_gkOA-rcK0
    - James Bond Goldfinger clip 2nd half only https://youtu.be/KZypBQC84HE
- James Bond sheet music http://www.007museum.com/James%20Bond%20-%20dr%20No.pdf
- Keyboards and headphones
- Various composing methods as available:
    - music notation or sequencer software
    - blank, lined or manuscript paper
    - classroom instruments and pupils' own instruments

Procedure

Starter - Appraising
- Teacher goes through assessment criteria and explains that the pupils' compositions will be marked out of 10 at the end of the lesson
- There should be a marked contrast in the given elements of music between the first and the second half of the clip

Main – Composing
- Pupils continue to compose on instruments/computers

Plenary – Performing
- All pupils perform their final composition, either on their instrument or on the computer

Film Music: assessment sheet

CLASS __ Name	Performing — James Bond					Composing — James Bond					Listening — Nov. exam					Comments
	Bass ostinato	Electric guitar riff	Trumpet tune	Hands together	Other	Tempo	Timbre	Dynamics	Tonality	Timing/effectiviess	Question 1	Question 2	Question 3	Question 4	TOTAL	

Caribbean Music

KS3 Scheme of Work – 6 lessons

Objectives

- To recognise and be able to perform offbeat and syncopated rhythms in calypso and reggae music
- To participate in a class performance of a calypso song using the steel pans
- To arrange own part in a reggae song for small ensemble performance
- To revise formation of chords made up of white notes (C, G)
- To learn formation of chords with a black note in the middle (D, E, A)

Lesson Overview

- Lesson 1: Calypso
- Lesson 2: Yellow Bird
- Lesson 3: offbeat
- Lesson 4: Riffs
- Lesson 5: Three Little Birds
- Lesson 6: Music of the Caribbean

Subject-specific vocabulary

- Instruments: steel pans, bass guitar, electric guitar, drums
- Rhythm: syncopation, offbeat
- Styles of music: calypso, reggae, soca, merengue

Assessments

- Performing (singing and steel pans) – 'Yellow Bird' (calypso)
- Arranging within a small ensemble – 'Three Little Birds' (reggae)
- Listening – Caribbean styles (calypso, reggae, soca, merengue)

Lesson 1: Calypso

Objective

- To learn about the distinctive 3+3+2 quaver pattern in calypso and apply this to a chord sequence

Resources

- Steel pans, or alternative instruments (metallophones, keyboards)
- Pupils' worksheets:
    - 'Calypso'
    - 'Steelpans'

Procedure

Starter – body percussion

- In pairs, learn the 3+3+2 calypso pattern by clapping own hands on the strong beats and partner's hands on the weak beats. Start slowly and increase the tempo until it becomes second nature.

Main – performing

- Set up steel pans (or alternative instruments) and stand in a horseshoe shape in the classroom
- Practise playing the chords G, D and C, in the following ways (if it gets too hard, pupils should stick with the level they are comfortable with)
    - Entry level: play the bass note only on the first beat of each bar
    - Basic level: play the bass line only on the three accented beats of each bard
    - Standard level: play two-note chords on the weak beats
    - Advanced level: play bass notes and two-note chords
- Chord sequence for 'Yellow Bird' (on powerpoint as well): GGDG GGDG CGDG CGDG

Plenary: performing on steel pans

- Run through, at a steady tempo, a class performance of the chord sequence for 'Yellow Bird'

Lesson 2: Yellow Bird

Objective
- To add the sung melody to the class calypso performance of 'Yellow Bird' and consolidate learning about steel pans and calypso

Resources
- Recording of sung version of 'Yellow Bird': https://www.youtube.com/watch?v=AifJ1HerRjI
- Lyrics for 'Yellow Bird': https://genius.com/Jessica-mauboy-yellow-bird-lyrics
- Steel pans (or alternative instruments)
- 'Steelpans' and 'Yellow Bird' worksheets

Procedure

Starter - listening
- Listen to recording of sung version of 'Yellow Bird'

Main - performing
- Learn to sing the melody of 'Yellow Bird' phrase by phrase (may be easier to sing in F)
- Set up instruments and stand in a horseshoe shape in the classroom
- Practise playing the chords G, D and C on the steelpans, differentiating as follows:
  - Entry level: play the bass note only on the first beat of each bar
  - Basic level: play the bass line only on the three accented beats of each bard
  - Standard level: play two-note chords on the weak beats
  - Advanced level: play bass notes and two-note chords
- Read chord sequence for 'Yellow Bird' from sheet music on worksheet (in G)

Plenary - performing
- Put together a class performance of 'Yellow Bird' with the sung melody and chord sequence on steelpans in calypso rhythm
- Teacher assesses each individual pupil's contribution to the class performance

Lesson 3: Three Little Chords

Objective
- To develop awareness of offbeat rhythms through singing and playing the chords for Bob Marley's song 'Three Little Birds'

Resources
- Recording of Bob Marley's song 'Three Little Birds': https://www.youtube.com/watch?v=zaGUr6wzyT8
- Lyrics for 'Three Little Birds': https://www.azlyrics.com/lyrics/bobmarley/threelittlebirds.html
- Pupils' worksheets for 'Three Little Chords' and 'Three Little Birds'
- Keyboards and headphones
- Unpitched percussion instruments

Procedure

Starter - listening
- Listen to Bob Marley's song 'Three Little Birds' and clap the offbeat rhythms

Main – performing
- As a class, learn to sing Bob Marley's song 'Three Little Birds' from lyrics on board
- Pupils read from worksheet 'Three Little Chords' that the song uses three chords: A major, D major and E major – the primary triads (I, IV and V) in the key of A major
- Pupils write out the fingers 1 3 5 on the keyboard diagrams on to show these three chords, observing that all three chords have the same pattern of white and black notes and hand shape
- Pupils go in pairs on keyboards to practise chords one at a time out loud as a class
- Pupils read the description of the chord sequence, then fill in the grid on the worksheet 'Three Little Birds'
- Pupils go in pairs on keyboards with headphones to practise chord sequence

Plenary – performing
- Some pairs of pupils demonstrate the chord sequence
- Whole class plays chord sequence out loud on offbeats, while singing 'Three Little Birds'

Lesson 4: Riffs

Objective
- To develop understanding of reggae by adding bass and melodic riffs to performance

Resources
- Worksheet of Bob Marley's song 'Three Little Birds' (filled in last lesson)
- Practice rooms
- Unpitched percussion instruments

Procedure

Starter: Singing
- Sing through Bob Marley's song 'Three Little Birds' using songsheet
- Learn to sing bass riff ('Who is the man? Bob Marley') and melodic riff ('Three Little Birds are singing')
- Combine the melody with both riffs as a class

Main: Performing
- Teacher demonstrates how to play the bass and the melodic riffs on the keyboard
- Individually or in pairs, practise playing bass line and/or offbeat chords on the keyboard, differentiating as follows:-
    - Basic level: play the bass line only on the beat
    - Standard level: play three-note chords on the offbeats
    - Advanced level: play bass line in left hand on the beat and chords in the right hand on the offbeats

Plenary: Performing
- Class performs Bob Marley's song 'Three Little Birds' with some pupils singing and others playing bass line and offbeat chords on the keyboards or on unpitched percussion instruments

- Teacher divides class into mixed-ability groups of 3-5 and explains that each group must arrange their own performance of Bob Marley's song 'Three Little Birds', including the following:
    - Sung melody
    - Bass riff
    - Offbeat chords
    - Melodic riff
    - (optional) Unpitched percussion instrument playing either on or off the beat
- Groups go into practice rooms and work on their arrangement together

Plenary: Performing
- Groups play work-in-progress to rest of class and teacher gives and invites feedback in order to refine performance for following lesson

Lesson 5: Three Little Birds

Objective
- To gain a practical understanding of the features of Reggae music through the ensemble performance of Bob Marley's song 'Three Little Birds' with singing, piano and percussion

Resources
- 3 or 4 practice rooms with pianos/keyboards
- 3 or 4 unpitched percussion instruments
- 'Three Little Birds' worksheet
- Recording device

Procedure

Starter - appraising
- Discuss and demonstrate what goes into the accompaniment for the song:
    - Riff, played at the top of the piano
    - offbeat chords, played in the middle of the piano
    - Syncopated bass line, played at the bottom of the piano
    - Unpitched percussion instrument playing either on or off the beat

Main
- Split into groups of 3-5 to rehearse as follows:
- Practise in practise rooms, with guidance from teacher. Aim to listen carefully to each other and maintain the challenging offbeat and syncopated rhythms

Plenary
- Perform 'Three Little Birds' to the class and record the work
- Teacher assesses each pupil's contribution to the small ensemble arrangement

Lesson 6: Caribbean Music

Objective
- To broaden understanding of Caribbean Music by listening to examples of soca, salsa and merengue in addition to the calypso and reggae styles already studied

Resources
- Worksheets on 'More Caribbean Music' and 'Listening to Caribbean Music'
- YouTube clips in different styles of Caribbean Music:
    - **Calypso** – 'Come Back Liza' by Harry Belafonte https://youtu.be/9GJ16klBPok
    - **Reggae** – 'Is this Love?' by Bob Marley https://youtu.be/CHekNnySAfM
    - **Soca** – 'Hot, Hot, Hot' by The Merrymen https://youtu.be/MYITD8TMvcM
    - **Salsa** – 'Que le ponga Salsa' by El Gran Combo https://youtu.be/ug1dCay4mjQ
    - **Merengue** – 'Sabina' by Pío Leiva https://youtu.be/migkOOkK_GE

Procedure

Starter: Appraising
- Read through the first two pages of the worksheet to find out more about Caribbean Music in general and the styles of soca, salsa and merengue in particular

Main: Listening
- Listen to five examples of Caribbean music and, on the third page of the worksheet, write down which style you think the music is in, from the following five options:
    - Calypso
    - Reggae
    - Soca
    - Salsa
    - Merengue
- Then write what musical features make you think the music is in this style.

Plenary: Appraising
- Listen to the recording of your group's arrangement of 'Three Little Birds' from last lesson

Caribbean Music Assessment Sheet

CLASS __ Name	Performing — *Yellow Bird*					Arranging — *Three Little Birds*					Listening — *Caribbean music*					Comments
	Maintains 3+3+2 calypso rhythm	Plays the bass line on the strong beats	Plays two-note chords on the weak beats	Rhythmic independence between hands	Sings melody	Performs an offbeat rhythmic pattern	Performs a melody or riff based on	Changes melody or riff when chord	Reacts and adjusts to other players	Maintains steady pulse throughout	Identifies Merengue style/features (qu1)	Identifies Soca style/features (qu2)	Identifies Salsa style/features (qu3)	Identifies Reggae style/features (qu4)	Identifies Calypso style/features (qu5)	

Indian Music

KS3 scheme of work

Objectives

- Performing: to play Indian ragas (melodic patterns) on the keyboard and to play talas (rhythmic cycles) on unpitched percussion
- Composing: to compose a raga for keyboard using black and white notes, with two-note drone
- Listening: to identify the following features of Indian classical music:
    - Timbre – Indian instruments: sitar, tabla and tambura
    - Melody – ragas (melodic patterns)
    - Rhythm – talas (rhythmic patterns)
    - Texture – layers of melody, drone and drum rhythm
    - Structure – sections of Indian classical piece: alap, jor and gat

Lesson overview

- Lesson 1: Instruments
- Lesson 2: Ragas
- Lesson 3: Composing your raga
- Lesson 4: Playing your raga
- Lesson 5: Talas
- Lesson 6: Further listening

Vocabulary

- Indian instruments:
    - SITAR
    - TABLA
    - TAMBURA
- Raga (melodic scale/pattern)
- Flats and sharps
- Tala (rhythmic cycle) vs. free rhythm (in alap)
- Improvisation
- Drone
- Structure: Alap, Jor, Gat

Assessment

- Performing: playing given raga on keyboard
- Composing: composing own raga on keyboard
- Listening: written exercise on Indian classical music

Lesson 1: Instruments

Objective

- To recognise three Indian instruments by sight and sound: sitar, tambura and tabla
- To understand the part each of these instruments plays within the texture of Indian classical music
- To learn the concept and notation of flats and sharps

Resources

- Pupil's worksheets: 'Instruments' and 'Flats and Sharps'
- Excerpt from raga: YouTube

Procedure

Starter: Listening

- Without the teacher announcing the piece, watch/listen to the YouTube video clip and answer the following questions orally:
    1. Where is this music from? (India.)
    2. What kind of instruments do you hear? (Plucked string instruments and hand drums.)
    3. What makes the tune sound different from more familiar music? (Different combinations of pitches/scales/white and black notes/'out of tune'.)

Main: Appraising

- Read the descriptions and label the pictures of the three instruments (top left – sitar, top right – tambura, bottom – tabla).
- Work out which function each instrument plays and label them accordingly (sitar – melody, tambura – drone, table – rhythm).
- Read the explanation on the worksheet 'Flats and sharps'.
- Write the letter-names of the white and black notes on the keyboard diagram.

Plenary: Listening and Appraising

- Pupils complete their written answers the Quick Quiz:

    1. Which instrument plays the drone in Indian music? TAMBURA

    2. What is the name of a black note to the left of a white note? FLAT

    3. How many strings does a sitar have? 20

    4. What is the name of the hand drums? TABLA

    5. What are the 'sharp' names of the three black notes grouped together on the keyboard? F#, G# and A#

Lesson 2: Ragas

Objectives

- To understand that a raga is the set of pitches used in a piece of Indian classical music (also called a raga)
- To play 1-5 raga(s) on the keyboard
- To recognise five different ragas by the number of different pitches and the combination of black and white notes

Resources

- Pupil's worksheet 'Ragas'
- Keyboards

Procedure

Starter: Appraising

- Teacher asks questions (without pupils referring to books) to consolidate last lesson's learning:
  - What are the three Indian instruments we learnt about? (Sitar, tambura and tabla.)
  - What is the function of each within Indian classical music? (Melody, drone and rhythm respectively.)
  - How exactly do we describe the black notes on a keyboard? (Flats and sharps – a flat is to the left of a white note and a sharp is to the right.)

Main: Appraising

- Read the explanation of 'Ragas' on the worksheet
- Write the letter-names below the notes for the five given ragas

Main: Performing

- Learn to play one or more of the five given ragas on the keyboard
- One pupil plays each raga to the rest of the class

Plenary: Listening

- Pupils listen to the five given ragas in a random order:
  - http://raag-hindustani.com/22_files/ArohBhupali.mp3 (Answer: Raga Bhopali)
  - http://raag-hindustani.com/22_files/AarohMarwaA.mp3 (Answer: Raga Marwa)
  - http://raag-hindustani.com/22_files/AarohBhairavA.mp3 (Answer: Raga Bhairav)
  - http://raag-hindustani.com/22_files/ArohShivaranjini.mp3 (Answer: Raga Shivaranjini)
  - http://raag-hindustani.com/22_files/AarohDurgaA.mp3 (Answer: Raga Durga)
- Pupils identify the ragas according to the number of different pitches and the combination of black and white notes

Lesson 3: Composing a raga

Objectives

- To compose a raga using a chosen combination of pitches (including black notes, for most pupils)

Resources

- Worksheet 'Composing a raga'
- Keyboards

Procedure

Starter: Listening

- Pupils refer to 'Ragas' worksheet while teacher plays the five ragas on a piano or keyboard
- What do these ragas have in common?
    - Each raga has 5-7 different notes
    - Each raga begins and ends on C
    - The notes are written and played in order of pitch
    - Some of the ragas use a combination of white and black notes
    - Each raga has a samay (time of day) and a rasa (mood)
- By the end of this lesson, each pupil should aim to compose a raga using a chosen combination of pitches (including black notes, for most pupils)

Main: Composing

- Pupils try out different combinations of pitches on the keyboard to create particular mood for a particular time of day.
- Pupils should use black notes as well as white notes if they can.
- When each pupil has chosen their 5-7 notes, they write the letter-names on the keyboard diagram below and, if they can, the notation on the stave below.
- When the raga is written down, if the pupils have time, they should practise playing the raga up and down.

Plenary: Performing

- Some pupils play their ragas up and down to the rest of the class.

Lesson 4: Playing your raga

Objectives

- To play chosen notes of own raga on the keyboard (including black notes, for most pupils)
- For many pupils to play in time with a given drum rhythm on the keyboard
- For some pupils to improvise using the notes of their raga

Resources

- YouTube video clip (1.09-4.00 approx.) Anoushka Shankar - Bhairavi - Live from Girona https://youtu.be/r97bzs3fyTY?t=1m9s
- Worksheet 'Composing a raga'
- Keyboards

Procedure

Starter: Listening

- Listen to an Indian classical raga and answer the following oral questions:
    - What happens at the beginning of the piece? (The RAGA is played up and down.)
    - What happens next? (The player IMPROVISES on the raga.)
    - What happens to the tempo when the drums come in? (It becomes REGULAR.)

Main: Composing

- Pupils go to the keyboards in pairs. The pupil on the right will develop their raga, while the pupil on the left will play a drone (a sustained/repeated low C). The pupils should swap places during their practice time.
- If necessary, pupils should finish writing the letter-names (and possibly the musical notation) for their raga.
- Pupils practise playing their raga up and down.
- Some pupils practise improvising on the notes of their raga.
- A few pupils play and/or improvise in time with a drum rhythm on the keyboard.
- Teacher assists and assesses pupils' compositions.

Plenary: Performing

- Most pupils play their ragas up and down to the rest of the class.
- Some pupils also improvise on the notes of their raga.

Lesson 5: Talas

Objectives
- To understand the variety of talas (rhythmic cycles) in Indian classical music
- To clap and count along with a variety of talas

Resources
- YouTube video Taal Keherva - Improvisation on Tabla
  https://www.youtube.com/watch?v=twuAbFLNhQA
- Worksheets 'Talas' and 'Performing Talas'
- A pair of tabla (if available) or another pair of hand drums (e.g. bongos)
- YouTube audio clips of different talas:
  1. Tin tal https://www.youtube.com/watch?v=IPGR0_PK2WE
  2. Ek tal https://www.youtube.com/watch?v=cnGc-poEc9E
  3. Kehrva tal https://www.youtube.com/watch?v=t_oy-vC6H1M
  4. Jhap tal https://www.youtube.com/watch?v=Zr3Xzs5uurg
  5. Rupak tal https://www.youtube.com/watch?v=kwc_vkUSSqc
  6. Dadra tal https://www.youtube.com/watch?v=b2m0YpI2Yek
  7. Dhamar tal https://www.youtube.com/watch?v=ZnuUiryMkXM

Procedure

Starter: Listening
- Watch YouTube video Taal Keherva - Improvisation on Tabla (at least the first 46 seconds) and answer the following questions:
  - What is the name of the drums the musician is playing? (TABLA.)
  - What are beat/rhythmic cycles called in Indian music? (TAAL or TALAS.)
  - What is the name of this beat cycle? (KEHERWA.)
  - How many beats are in this cycle? (EIGHT.)

Main: Performing
- Pupils read through the information on 'Talas' and try clapping the Tintal (16-beat cycle).
- Pupils clap along to tabla improvisations on various talas.

Plenary: Composing
- Some pupils take turns in improvising their own rhythms on various talas clapped by the rest of the class.

Lesson 6: Further listening

Objectives
- To listen to Bhangra and understand how this style has fused with Western popular styles such as hip-hop
- To demonstrate learning in a listening exercise on Indian classical music

Resources
- YouTube audio clip for Bhangra Paundi | PBN & Manpreet Toor (Feat. Sharky P)
  https://www.youtube.com/watch?v=DhAl2IMX0ks
- Unseen assessment sheet 'Listening to Indian music'
- YouTube audio clips for listening exercise
    - Ravi Shankar - Raga Rageshri: Pt. 1 (Alap)
      https://www.youtube.com/watch?v=SmPaHSOODwo
    - Ravi Shankar - Raga Rageshri: Pt. 2 (Jor)
      https://www.youtube.com/watch?v=LsdDhb6qii0
    - Ravi Shankar - Raga Rageshri: Pt. 3 (Gat)
      https://www.youtube.com/watch?v=xKwQ7UJrpRc

Procedure

Starter: Listening
- Listen to a Bhangra song and discuss the Indian and Western influences on this style of music.

Main: Listening
- Pupils read through the worksheet entitled 'Bhangra'
- Pupils listen to the same Bhangra song from the beginning of the lesson.
- For each feature of music, pupils make notes on Indian and Western influences.

Plenary: Listening
- Pupils complete unseen unseen assessment sheet 'Listening to Indian music'.

Listening to Indian Music

Extracts A, B, C: Raga Rageshri by Ravi Shankar

Choose the answers for questions 1-9 from the box below.

| flute - brass - louder - sitar - woodwind - drone - guitar |
| in stricter time - strings - faster - tambura – banjo - raga |
| freer - quieter - higher- lower- slower - improvisation |

1. Which instrument is playing the melody?.. [1]

2. What instrument is playing the drone accompaniment? .... [1]

3. What instrument is playing the drum rhythm in Extract C only?................................... [1]

4. What is the name of the basic melodic pattern used in this piece? .... [1]

5. What is the name of the rhythmic cycle played by the drums?..................................... [1]

6. What word describes making up music during a performance? .... [1]

7. Extract A is from the beginning of the piece. What is this section called? .... [1]

8. Extract B comes later, before the drums come in. What is this section called? .... [1]

9. Extract C is accompanied by the drums. What is this section called? .... [1]

10. Give THREE reasons why Indian music is different from Western music..................................
....
.... [3]

11. Do you like or dislike Indian music? Give a musical reason why (not). ....
....
.... [3]

TOTAL [15]

Indian Music: assessment sheet

CLASS __	Performing given raga	Composing own raga	Listening to Indian Music	Comments
Name	Plays white notes from letter-names / Plays black notes from letter-names / Plays white notes from notation / Plays black notes from notation / Plays fluently, with a sense of pulse	Writes white and black letter-names correctly / Notates white and black notes correctly / Plays raga up and down in free time / Improvises using notes of own raga / Plays in time with a drum rhythm	Identifies instruments (qus 1-3) / Identifies main features (4-6) / Idenfities structural features (7-9) / Compares music from different cultures (qu 10) / Expresses/justifies opinions about music (qu 11)	

101

Classical Music

Scheme of Work (6-8 lessons)

Objectives

- To learn about different genres, composers, instruments and musical forms from the Classical Era (1750-1820),
- To apply this knowledge when listening to an unfamiliar piece
- To sing both a song and an opera aria from the Classical Era
- To understand how both accompanying patterns and melodies can be created from notes in the underlying chords (using the major triads G, D, A, C and F)
- As a result, to be able to play both an accompanying ('oom-cha') pattern and a melody (for a minuet) on the keyboard
- To compose one or two 8-bar section(s) of music, using chords and melody, which can be used as another section of a minuet in either ternary or Rondo form

Lesson Overview

- Lesson 1: Schubert's 'The Trout' and Strophic Form
- Lesson 2: Gluck's 'What is life' and Rondo form
- Lesson 3: Consolidation of Classical Vocal music
- Lesson 4: Haydn's 'Emperor Quartet' and Variation form
- Lesson 5: Mozart's Minuet and Ternary Form
- Lesson 6: Consolidation of musical forms
- Lesson 7: Beethoven's Fifth Symphony and Sonata Form*
- Lesson 8: Conclusion*

* Optional lessons which may be omitted for a six-lesson scheme of work

Subject-specific vocabulary

- Composers: Schubert, Gluck, Mozart, Haydn, Beethoven
- Genres: song, opera, aria, symphony, minuet
- Voices, instruments and their groupings: soprano, alto, piano, string quartet, orchestra
- Forms: strophic, rondo, ternary, theme and variations, sonata form

Assessments

- Performing (singing) – Schubert's 'The Trout' or Gluck's 'What is life'
- Performing (keyboard) – adaptations of accompaniment to 'The Trout' or Mozart's Minuet
- Composing – additional 8-bar section(s) for Mozart's Minuet
- Listening – exercise on unfamiliar piece in last lesson

Lesson 1: Schubert's 'The Trout' and Strophic Form

Objectives
- To sing a Classical song in strophic form
- To understand how both accompanying ('oom-cha') pattern can be created from notes in the underlying chords (using the major triads G, D, A, C and F) and to play it on the keyboard

Resources
- Pupils' worksheets: 'Chords for The Trout' and 'The Trout'
- Keyboards, headphones and splitters

Procedure

Starter: Performing (singing)
- Warm up voices and learn to sing, phrase by phrase, Schubert's song 'The Trout' from worksheet

Main: Performing (keyboard)
- Watch the teacher demonstrate the four triads (three-note chords) used in 'The Trout' (G, D, A and C major) and write down the notes used on the worksheet 'Chords for The Trout', both as letter-names and on the keyboard diagrams
- On keyboards, mostly in pairs, play the four chords as a class, without headphones to begin with. The task can be differentiated as follows:
    - Less able pupils play only the bass line (i.e. the first note/root of each chord) on the left hand side of the keyboard
    - More able pupils have a keyboard to themselves and play chords and bass line together with both hands
- Watch the teacher demonstrate the chord sequence from the 4x5 grid on the worksheet 'Chords for The Trout': four crotchets per bar, notes and bass line together
- On keyboards, mostly in pairs, practise the chord sequence, using headphones and splitters. The task can be differentiated as follows:
    - Less able pupils play only the bass line (i.e. the first note/root of each chord) on the left hand side of the keyboard
    - More able pupils have a keyboard to themselves and play chords and bass line together with both hands
- Watch the teacher demonstrate the chord sequence, this time alternating the crotchet bass line and chords in an 'oom-cha' pattern (like the accompaniment on the sheet music, although the triad does not have to be split in exactly the same way: it can be done with bass line and complete triad an octave apart)
- On keyboards, mostly in pairs, practise the chord sequence in an 'oom-cha' pattern, using headphones and splitters. The task can be differentiated as follows:
    - Less able pupils play only the bass line (i.e. the first note/root of each chord) on the left hand side of the keyboard

- - More able pupils have a keyboard to themselves and play chords and bass line together with both hands
- While the pupils are practising, the teacher can begin to assess their performance on the assessment sheets provided

Plenary: Performing (keyboard)

- Some/all pupils (at teacher's discretion) demonstrate their work to the rest of the class

Lesson 2: Gluck's 'What is life' and Rondo form

Objectives
- To learn about the genre of opera and Rondo form
- To sing a Classical opera
- To understand how both accompanying ('oom-cha') pattern can be created from notes in the underlying chords (using the major triads G, D, A, C and F) and to play it on the keyboard

Resources
- Pupils' worksheets:
    - 'Opera and Rondo form'
    - 'Chords for The Trout' (completed last lesson)
    - 'The Trout' (from last lesson)
- Keyboards and headphones

Procedure

Starter: Performing (singing)
- Pupils read through worksheet 'Opera and Rondo form' about Gluck reformed opera in the Classical Era. Discuss his quote from the Preface to his opera Alceste on the sheet music.
- Warm up voices and learn to sing, phrase by phrase, Gluck's ARIA 'What is life' from sheet music. How would you describe the FORM of the aria? (ABACA – Rondo form)

Main: Performing (keyboard)
- Watch the teacher demonstrate the chord sequence for 'The Trout' in an 'oom-cha' pattern (as a reminder of last lesson's work)
- On keyboards, mostly in pairs, practise the chord sequence in an 'oom-cha' pattern, using headphones and splitters. The task can be differentiated as follows:
    - Less able pupils play only the bass line (i.e. the first note/root of each chord) on the left hand side of the keyboard
    - More able pupils have a keyboard to themselves and play chords and bass line together with both hands
- While the pupils are practising, the teacher can complete the assessment of their performance on the assessment sheets provided
- Some/all pupils (at teacher's discretion) demonstrate their work to the rest of the class

Plenary: Listening

- To listen to recordings of both pieces, giving oral responses about the voice type, accompaniment, form and how the recordings are different from the versions the pupils learnt to sing.

	Schubert's song 'The Trout'	**Gluck's aria 'What is life'**
YouTube link	http://www.youtube.com/watch?v=Vpe253nlj9w	http://www.youtube.com/watch?v=qQuahSdTvU4
Voice type	Soprano [Lucia Popp]	(Contr)alto [Kathleen Ferrier]
Accompaniment	Piano	Orchestra
Form	Strophic	Rondo
Differences	Additional sextuplet figure in piano accompaniment; third verse departs from strophic form as the trout is caught	Same version musically, although the pupils may comment about the operatic style of singing

Lesson 3: Consolidation of Classical Vocal Music

Objectives

- To consolidate knowledge of Classical opera and song
- To sing or accompany a piece of Classical vocal music
- To understand how both accompanying ('oom-cha') pattern can be created from notes in the underlying chords (using the major triads G, D, A, C and F) and to play it on the keyboard

Resources

- Pupils' worksheets from last lesson:
    - 'Opera and Rondo form'
    - 'Chords for The Trout'
    - 'The Trout'
- Keyboards and headphones

Procedure

Starter: Performing (singing)

- Warm up voices and sing through both Schubert's 'The Trout' and Gluck's 'What is life'. Briefly recap the differences between the two (voice types, accompaniment and form).

Main: Performing (singing)

- Individually or in pairs, pupils choose either Schubert's 'The Trout' and Gluck's 'What is life' to sing to the rest of the class.
- Accompanied by the teacher, pupils sing their chosen song or aria individually or in pairs. This is assessed by the teacher using the assessment sheet provided.

Performing: (singing and keyboard)

- The teacher divides the class into small groups of 2, 3, or 4. This should be based on the best combination of abilities, both in singing and on the keyboard, so that there are one or two pupils singing 'The Trout' and one or two pupils accompanying it on the keyboard using the 'oom-cha' accompaniment in each group.
- The small groups go to practice rooms and other breakout areas to practise 'The Trout', monitored by the teacher.

Plenary: Performing (singing and keyboard)

- The small groups perform their work-in-progress to the rest of the class. (The teacher may use the opportunity to add any further observations to the pupils' singing or keyboard assessment.)

Lesson 4: Haydn's 'Emperor Quartet' and Variation form

Objectives

- To learn about the composer Haydn, Theme and Variations and the string quartet
- To apply this knowledge when listening to Haydn's 'Emperor' quartet variations
- To understand how both accompanying ('oom-cha') pattern can be created from notes in the underlying chords (using the major triads G, D, A, C and F) and to play it on the keyboard

Resources

- Pupils' worksheets:
    - 'Chords for The Trout' (from previous lessons)
    - 'The Trout' (from previous lessons)
    - 'Franz Joseph Haydn'
- Practice rooms and other breakout areas
- A packet of Smarties or Skittles
- YouTube link for Haydn's 'Emperor' Theme and Variations:
  https://www.youtube.com/watch?v=L_chH88_--A

Procedure

Starter – Performing (singing and keyboard)

- The class divides into the same small groups of 2, 3, or 4 as they did in the last lesson. There should still be one or two pupils singing 'The Trout' and one or two pupils accompanying it on the keyboard using the 'oom-cha' accompaniment in each group.
- The small groups go to practice rooms and other breakout areas to practise 'The Trout', monitored by the teacher.
- The small groups perform to the rest of the class. (The teacher may use the opportunity to add any further observations to the pupils' singing or keyboard assessment.)

Main - Appraising

- Read and discuss the information about Haydn, String Quartet and Variations form on the worksheet

Plenary - Listening

- As the pupils listen to the 'Emperor' theme and its four variations, they secretly show the teacher the correct coloured Skittle for each section as it is playing. If they chose the correct colour, they can eat it. (If not, they get another chance.)
- *Order of correct answers: Orange, green, yellow, red, purple.*

Lesson 5: Mozart's Minuet and Ternary Form

Objectives
- To learn about Mozart and ternary form
- To be able to play a minuet melody on the keyboard
- To understand how melodies can be created from notes in the underlying chords (using the major triads G, D, A, C and F)
- To compose one or two 8-bar section(s) of music, using chords and melody, which can be used as another section of a minuet in either ternary or Rondo form

Resources
- Pupils' worksheets: 'Wolfgang Amadeus Mozart' and 'Composing a Minuet'
- Keyboards, headphones and splitters
- Mozart's minuet, K.2 https://www.youtube.com/watch?v=KLybPeqm3uY

Procedure

Starter - Listening
- Pupils read through worksheet 'Wolfgang Amadeus Mozart'
- Listen to the teacher play Mozart's Minuet, K.2. What musical form is it in? (ABA or Ternary)
- Teacher demonstrates chords C, F and G on the keyboard while pupils refer to worksheet 'Composing a Minuet'

Main – Composing
- On the keyboards, mostly in pairs, play the three chords C, F and G as a class, without headphones to begin with. Try to read the notes at the top of the worksheet whilst playing the chords. The task can be differentiated as follows:
  - Less able pupils play only the bass line (i.e. the first note/root of each chord) on the left hand side of the keyboard
  - More able pupils have a keyboard to themselves and play chords and bass line together with both hands
- Write a chord symbol (C, F or G) in each box above the first four bars by looking carefully at the notes in the melody, playing the notes (with headphones) and working out which chord they come from (answer: C, F, C, G).
- Now work out melody for the next four bars by reversing the above process: look at the chords (C, F, G, C) and write down the notes in the same rhythm of two quavers and two crotchets (with a dotted minim in bar 8). The pitches come from the underlying chord in this order: middle, top, bottom, bottom. (Answer: EGCC/ACFF/BDGG/C)
- The teacher begins to assess the pupils' composing skills on the assessment sheets provided
- Practice playing the first eight bars of the Minuet. The task can be differentiated as follows:
  - Less able pupils play only the bass line (i.e. the first note/root of each chord for a whole bar) on the left hand side of the keyboard

- Pupils of average ability can accompany the minuet by creating a broken chord from the triads in crotchets (bottom-middle-top)
- More able pupils have a keyboard to themselves and play chords and bass line together with both hands

Plenary: Composing

- Some/all pupils (at teacher's discretion) demonstrate their work to the rest of the class. This may show the project at different stages: some pupils may play just the chord sequence, others may play the melody.

Lesson 6: Consolidation of musical forms

Objectives

- To consolidate knowledge of Classical forms: strophic, ternary, rondo, and theme and variations
- To compose one or two 8-bar section(s) of music, using chords and melody, which can be used as another section of a minuet in either ternary or Rondo form

Resources

- A packet of Liquorice Allsorts
- Recordings of 'The Trout', 'What is Life', 'Minuet K.2' and the 'Emperor' Variations
- Keyboards with headphones and splitters
- Pupils' worksheets: 'Wolfgang Amadeus Mozart' and 'Composing a Minuet'

Procedure

Starter - Listening

- Start by recapping the four musical forms studied so far in this Classical Era project. Explain that different musical forms are like different Liquorice Allsorts:
    - Strophic Form (AAAA...) is like the solid liquorice sweets – the same all the way through
    - Ternary Form (ABA) is like the single 'sandwich' sweets – the same colour on the outside, but different colour in the middle
    - Rondo Form (ABACA) is like the double 'sandwich' sweets – the same colour on the outside and the middle, but separated by layers of different colours
    - Theme and Variations (AA1A2A3...) as well as being like Smarties or Skittles, are also like those pink or blue jelly sweets covered in little balls.
- If the pupils can work out the correct musical form of three pieces they have already studied, they can have a Liquorice Allsort. Without the titles or composers being announced, listen to recordings (in a random order) of 'The Trout', 'What is Life', 'Minuet K.2' and the 'Emperor' Variations.
- After the teacher has played enough of the piece for the form to be clear, the pupils have three options: strophic, ternary, rondo or variations. They put up their hand for what they think is the answer. The correct answer is rewarded with a Liquorice Allsort (it does not have to be the same type - maximum one sweet per pupil).

Main – Composing

- Continue composing the first eight bars of the Minuet (see last lesson plan). When the pupils have completed this, they can start composing the next eight bars:
    - First, choose a chord (C, F or G) for each bar and write it in the boxes provided. Avoid using F at the end of each four-bar phrases (this will result in either an imperfect cadence, if the last chord of the phrase is G, or a perfect cadence, if the last chord of the phrase is C).

111

- - Then, write a melody using the notes in the underlying chords and the same rhythms as the first eight bars. (If they finish this, they can write another eight-bars to create a C section.)
- Practice playing the Minuet in ternary (or rondo) form. The task can be differentiated as follows:
  - Less able pupils play only the bass line (i.e. the first note/root of each chord for a whole bar) on the left hand side of the keyboard
  - Pupils of average ability can accompany the minuet by creating a broken chord from the triads in crotchets (bottom-middle-top)
  - More able pupils have a keyboard to themselves and play chords and bass line together with both hands
- While the pupils are practising, the teacher can continue to assess their composing on the assessment sheets provided

Plenary: Composing

- Some/all pupils (at teacher's discretion) demonstrate their work to the rest of the class

Lesson 7: Beethoven's Fifth Symphony and Sonata Form

Objectives

- To learn about the Classical Orchestra and Sonata Form
- To compose one or two 8-bar section(s) of music, using chords and melody, which can be used as another section of a minuet in either ternary or Rondo form

Resources

- YouTube video: Beethoven Symphony 5 Movement I (Annotated Analysis) (https://www.youtube.com/watch?v=br1EMrlGXyw)
- Pupil's worksheets:
    - 'The Classical Orchestra'
    - 'Composing a Minuet'
- Sonata form: a musical jigsaw (single page worksheet) *NB. This is included in the teacher's notes, rather than the pupil's workbook, as it needs to be photocopied and cut out*
- Scissors and glue for each pupil
- Assessment sheet

Procedure

Starter – appraising

- Pupils look at the diagram of the Classical orchestra and complete the table underneath

Main - listening

- Teacher explains that the first movement of Beethoven's 5th symphony is in **Sonata Form** and that the pupils are going to work out how this is put together using their musical jigsaws.
- Pupils cut up their jigsaws using scissors.
- Listen to the first movement of Beethoven's 5th symphony with annotated analysis on video and arrange the jigsaw pieces in the correct order.
- Go over correct answer and stick the jigsaw pieces onto the plain paper in the correct order.

Main: Composing

- The teacher distributes the pupils' folders with the 'Mozart's Minuet' worksheet and directs pupils to their composing task as follows:
- First, choose a chord (C, F or G) for each bar and write it in the boxes provided. Avoid using F at the end of each four-bar phrases (this will result in either an imperfect cadence, if the last chord of the phrase is G, or a perfect cadence, if the last chord of the phrase is C).
- Then, write a melody using the notes in the underlying chords and the same rhythms as the first eight bars. (If they finish this, they can write another eight-bars to create a C section.)
- Practice playing the Minuet in ternary (or rondo) form. The task can be differentiated as follows:
    - Less able pupils play only the bass line (i.e. the first note/root of each chord for a whole bar) on the left hand side of the keyboard

- - Pupils of average ability can accompany the minuet by creating a broken chord from the triads in crotchets (bottom-middle-top)
  - More able pupils have a keyboard to themselves and play chords and bass line together with both hands
- While the pupils are practising, the teacher can complete the assessment of their composing on the assessment sheets provided

Plenary: Composing

- Some/all pupils (at teacher's discretion) demonstrate their work to the rest of the class

Lesson 8: Conclusion

Objectives

- To apply the knowledge learnt throughout the topic when listening to an unfamiliar piece
- To use practical skills (performing and composing) to demonstrate different musical forms

Resources

- Listening exercise (double-sided worksheet) NB. This is included in the teacher's notes, as it is an unseen listening exercise
- YouTube video: Schubert 'Trout' Quintet Movement IV
  https://www.youtube.com/watch?v=HwbWvGtaZGo
- Pupils' worksheet 'Composing a Minuet'

Procedure

Starter

- The teacher leads oral questioning and discussion on the composers, genres, timbres and forms studied in this project:-
  - Composers: Schubert, Gluck, Mozart, Haydn, Beethoven
  - Genres: song, opera, aria, symphony, minuet
  - Voices, instruments and their groupings: soprano, alto, piano, string quartet, orchestra
  - Forms: strophic, rondo, ternary, theme and variations, sonata form

Main: Listening

- Distribute listening exercise (double-sided worksheet)
- The teacher plays the video (try to avoid announcing the piece or composer, or showing title at the very beginning; this gives away some of the answers)
- Pupils complete listening exercise
- (after lesson) Teacher assesses listening exercise, completing assessment sheet for each pupil

Plenary: Composing and Performing

- The class is going to finish by demonstrating some of the musical forms by playing different versions of Mozart's Minuet.
- Some pupils (pairs or individuals) are chosen by the teacher to play the first eight bars of 'Mozart's Minuet' on the keyboard. (These pupils are chosen because their performance of the first eight bars is stronger than their composition.) Collectively, these pupils will demonstrate **Strophic Form.**
- Then another pair/individual are invited by the teacher to play the first eight bars of 'Mozart's Minuet', followed by another pair/individual playing an 8-bar section that one of them composed, followed by another pair/individual playing the original 8 bars. Collectively, these pupils will demonstrate **Ternary Form.**
- Finally, another group of pairs/individuals play in the order ABACA (A being the original 8 bars, B and C being composed sections) to create **Rondo Form.**
- A particularly able pair/individual may be confident enough to demonstrate a whole ternary or even rondo form by themselves.

Che farò senza Euridice?

What is life to me without thee?
ARIA (Orfeo)

English text: Claude Aveling

Christoph Willibald Gluck (1714-1787)

17
Eu-ri - di - ce! Eu-ri - di - ce! Oh Di - o! Ri -
Eu-ri - di - ce! Eu-ri - di - ce! Ah, hear me! Make
21
Adagio
spon-di! Ri - spon - - - - di! I - o son
an - swer! Make an - - - - swer! Thy dear
cresc.
25
poco rit.
pu - re il tu-o fe - de - le, son pu - re il tu-o fe - de - le, il tuo fe -
lord am I so faith-ful, thy faith - ful lord who lo-ves thee, who doth
29
Tempo I.
de - le, Che fa-rò sen-za Eu-ri - di - ce? do-ve an-drò sen-za il mio ben? Che fa -
love thee! What is life to me with-out thee? What is left if thou art dead? What is

34
cresc.
f
rò ___ do - ve an - drò ___ che fa - rò __ sen - za il mi - o ben, __ do - ve an-
life, ___ life _ with - out thee? What is ___ life, with - out _ my ___ love? _ What is ___
sf
sf
f
38
dim. e rall.
Moderato.
f
Adagio
drò sen - za il mi - o ben? Eu - ri - di - ce! Eu - ri - di - ce! Ah! non m'a-
life if ___ thou art _ dead? Eu - ri - di - ce! Eu - ri - di - ce! In my dread
dim. e rall.
mf
43
van - za più ___ soc - cor - so, più ___ spe - ran - za, nè dal mon - do, nè ___ dal
am - guish none _ can com - fort, none _ can aid me. Earth is cru - el, heaven is
fp
f
48
Tempo I.
p
ciel! Che fa - rò sen - za Eu - ri - di - ce? do - ve an - drò sen - za il mio ben? _ Che fa -
cold! What is life to me with - out thee? What is left if thou art dead? What is _
p
fp

53
rò ___ do - ve an - drò ___ che fa - rò ___ sen - za il mi - o ben, ___ do - ve an-
life, ___ life ___ with - out thee? What is ___ life, with - out ___ my ___ love? ___ What is ___
sf
sf
mf
57
p
cresc.
f
drò ___ che fa - rò, ___ che fa - rò ___ sen - za il mi - o ben, sen -
life, ___ life ___ with - out thee? What is ___ life ___ if ___ thou art ___ dead, if ___
cresc.
p
cresc.
f
61
ff
f
ritenuto
za il mi - o ben, ___ sen - za il mi - o ben?
thou art dead, ___ if ___ thou art dead?
ff
rit. colla voce
cresc.
66
cresc.
sf
sf

Mozart's Minuet

Sonata Form: a musical jigsaw

For this exercise, you will need scissors and glue.

Cut out the 18 jigsaw pieces opposite.

Watch the video clip of Beethoven's Fifth Symphony (1st movement).

As you watch and listen, arrange the jigsaw pieces on the back of the 'Classical Orchestra' worksheet so that:

- The three main sections of sonata form are shown in order across the top row of the grid
- The shorter sections of section form are shown in order across the bottom row of the grid

When you have checked the answer with the teacher, glue the jigsaw pieces onto the back of your worksheet.

EXPOSITION			DEVELOPMENT	RECAPITULATION			
							Coda
1st subject (home key)	Bridge passage ending in different key	2nd subject (different key)	Codetta	1st and/or 2nd subject(s) transformed in different keys	1st subject (home key)	Bridge passage ending in home key	2nd subject (home key)

Classical Music Listening Exercise

Listen to an extract of music THREE times. The extract lasts for about two minutes and contains three sections of roughly equal length.

Answer the questions below by circling the correct letter (a-e).

1. Which era of Music History was this piece written in?
   a. Renaissance
   b. Baroque
   c. Classical
   d. Romantic
   e. Modern

2. The composer based this on one of his other pieces. Which is it?
   a. The Trout
   b. What is Life
   c. Minuet
   d. Hymn to the Emperor
   e. Symphony No. 5

3. Who is the composer?
   a. Mozart
   b. Gluck
   c. Schubert
   d. Haydn
   e. Beethoven

4. What ensemble (group) plays in the first section?
   a. Orchestra
   b. Choir
   c. Brass quartet
   d. Wind quartet
   e. String quartet

5. Which instrument plays the tune in the FIRST section?
   a. Flute
   b. Oboe
   c. Violin
   d. Guitar
   e. Trumpet

6. Which instrument plays the tune in the SECOND section?
    a. Guitar
    b. Piano
    c. Harpsichord
    d. Harp
    e. Organ

7. Which instrument plays the tune in the THIRD section?
    a. Trombone
    b. Tuba
    c. Clarinet
    d. Viola
    e. Double bass

8. Which of the following instruments is also playing in this piece?
    a. 'Cello
    b. Timpani
    c. Piccolo
    d. Bassoon
    e. French horn

9. What form is this piece in?
    a. Strophic
    b. Rondo
    c. Ternary
    d. Variations
    e. Sonata

10. What is the best description of this whole ensemble?
    a. Duet
    b. Trio
    c. Quartet
    d. Quintet
    e. Sextet

11. Do you like this piece? Give a musical reason why (not).

....

....

....

Total out of 12:____

Answers

Sonata form jigsaw

EXP	OSI	TION		DEV	ELOP	MENT	REC	APITU	LATION	
1st subject (home key)	Bridge passage ending in different key	2nd subject (different key)	Codetta	1st and/or 2nd subject(s) transformed in different keys			1st subject (home key)	Bridge passage ending in home key	2nd subject (home key)	Coda

Listening Exercise

1. c Classical
2. a The Trout
3. c Schubert
4. e String Quartet (although this piece uses a different combination of instruments from the normal string quartet of two violins, viola and 'cello: this piece uses violin, viola, 'cello and double bass)
5. c Violin
6. b Piano
7. d Viola
8. a 'Cello
9. d Variations
10. d Quintet
11. No credit for liking or disliking the music; one mark for referring to a musical element (pitch, tempo, texture, dynamics, timbre, duration, structure) and one mark for describing it appropriately (e.g. pitch=high/low, tempo=slow/fast etc.

Classical Music: Assessment Sheet

CLASS __ Name	Performing *Singing/playing Schubert's 'Trout'* Maintains strong sense of pulse / Correct rhythms / Correct pitches/intonation / Sings from memory OR plays bass and chords / Performs with style and confidence	Composing *Middle section of Mozart's 'Minuet'* Effective chord progression with cadences / Each bar has three beats / Variety of rhythm / Melody based on underlying chords / Suitable melodic shape and range	Listening *Schubert's 'Trout Quintet'* Identifies correct era and piece (qu1,2) / Identifies composer and ensemble (qu3,4) / Identifies solo instruments (qu5,6) / Identifies other instruments (qu 7,8) / Identifies form and tempo (qu 9,10)	Comments

Jazz

KS3 Scheme of Work – 6 lessons

Objectives

- To listen to different styles of jazz and its influences: Blues, Ragtime, New Orleans Jazz, Swing Era big bands, Bebop, latin jazz, and rock fusion
- To sing songs a spiritual and blues song in the jazz style, both in class and individually
- To develop improvising skills using a variety of scales and note patterns (rhythm only, pentatonic minor scale, five notes (C-G), blues scale, chord notes) on given tunes and chord sequences

Lesson outline

- Lesson 1 – Blues and Ragtime
- Lesson 2 – New Orleans Jazz
- Lesson 3 – The Swing Era
- Lesson 4 – Later Jazz Styles
- Lesson 5 – When the Saints go Marching In
- Lesson 6 – Improvising Assessment

Subject-specific vocabulary

- **Instruments** – piano, drum kit, double bass, trumpet, cornet, clarinet, trombone, saxophone, banjo
- **Blues notes** – where some notes have a slightly lower pitch
- **Call-and-response** – where the lead singer's phrases are echoed by other singers or instruments
- **Major scale** – an ordinary seven-note scale in a major key
- **Oom-pah accompaniment** – a backing pattern where bass notes alternate with chords, all on the beat
- **Syncopated** – where the offbeat notes are accented
- **Swing** – where the beat is divided unequally into a long note and a short note
- **Rhythm section** keeps the beat and accompanies with bass line and chords
- **Frontline instruments** play the original melody (**head**) and **improvise**
- **Improvise** - make up the music as you go along
- **Head** – the original, composed melody of a particular song
- **Scat singing**
- **Walking bass**
- **'Ten-to-ten' rhythm** – repeated crotchet and two swung quavers on ride cymbal

Assessments

- Performing: playing 'In the Mood' on the keyboard (Lesson 3)
- Listening: listening exercise on 'When the Saints Go Marching In' (Lesson 5)
- Composing: improvising on 'When the Saints Go Marching In' (Lesson 6)

Lesson 1 – Blues and Ragtime

Objectives

- To recognise the features of blues and ragtime that influenced New Orleans (traditional) jazz
- To develop rhythmic skills in performing and improvising

Resources

- Pupils' worksheet: 'Blues and Ragtime'
- YouTube clips:
    - Blues: 'Thinking Blues' by Bessie Smith https://youtu.be/MzLri6gt5ig
    - Ragtime: 'Pineapple Rag' by Scott Joplin https://youtu.be/3-PtpGBmr5E
- Unpitched classroom percussion instruments
- Piano or guitar for teacher

Procedure

Starter – listening

- Pupils read through first paragraph on the worksheet 'Blues and Ragtime' and go through the list of musical features in bold
- Pupils listen to 'Thinking Blues' and 'Pineapple Rag', completing table of musical features
- Teacher goes through answers with class:

	Thinking Blues *by Bessie Smith*	**Pineapple Rag** *by Scott Joplin*
TIMBRE	Voice, trumpet, piano	Piano
RHYTHM	Swing (also syncopated)	Syncopated
TEXTURE	Call-and-response	Oom-pah accompaniment
MELODY	Blue notes	Major scale

Main – performing

- Teacher claps a series of two-bar swung and syncopated rhythms which are copied by the whole class
- Teacher claps similar rhythms which, in response, are improvised on collectively by the whole class
- Teacher claps similar rhythms which, in response, are improvised on individually by the whole class
- Repeat the above with unpitched classroom percussion instruments instead of clapping

Plenary – performing

- Teacher explains that now the class will put this rhythmic call-and-response/improvisation into a 12-bar blues structure
- Teacher demonstrates a two-bar swung and syncopated rhythm which the pupils copy – this is to be played for the first two bars of each four-bar 'line' of the 12-bar blues
- Teacher plays 12-bar blues on piano or guitar; the pupils play the given rhythm for the first two bars of each line, then pupils take turn to improvise a response for the second half of each line

Lesson 2 – New Orleans Jazz

Objectives

- To listen to an example of New Orleans Jazz, identifying the influences of Blues and Ragtime, identifying the instruments, and analysing its repeated 12-bar blues structure, with both collective and individual improvisation
- To practise collective and individual improvisation on a pentatonic minor scale

Resources

- Pupils' worksheets on 'New Orleans jazz'
- YouTube recording of King Oliver's Creole Jazz Band's 'Dippermouth Blues': https://youtu.be/BEF9QeHxrYw
- Keyboards
- Piano or guitar for teacher

Procedure

Starter – listening

- Pupils listen to recording of King Oliver's Creole Jazz Band's 'Dippermouth Blues'
- Teacher tells them this is the original style of jazz, 'New Orleans Jazz' (also known as 'Trad Jazz' or 'Dixieland') and asks what musical features they recognise from Blues and Ragtime (swing and syncopated rhythms, blue notes, 12-bar blues structure, call-and-response etc.)

Main – listening

- Pupils read about King Oliver's Creole Jazz Band
- Pupils listen to 'Dippermouth Blues' again and identify the instruments, categorising them either as 'frontline' or 'rhythm section':
    - Frontline – trumpet, cornet, clarinet, trombone
    - Rhythm section – drum kit, double bass, piano, banjo
- Pupils read about the Structure of Jazz on the worksheet
- Pupils listen to 'Dippermouth Blues' again and identify the instruments playing the solos (clarinet and cornet, although 'trumpet' is an acceptable answer for the latter)

Plenary – improvising

- Teacher explains that the class is going to improvise on a 12-bar blues, New Orleans style
- Teacher explains that the improvisation is based on the black note on the keyboard, with Eb as the key note (i.e. Eb pentatonic minor)
- Teacher invites all pupils to improvise collectively and volunteers to improvise solos and writes the structure of the piece on the board
- Teacher plays a 12-bar blues in Eb on the piano or guitar
- All pupils improvise collectively for the 'head' at the beginning and end of the piece and some pupils improvise 12-bar solos in the middle
- Teacher can support the pupil soloists by playing two-bar 'call' at the beginning of each line, to which the pupils gives a two-bar 'response'
- More able pupil soloists can structure their 12-bar solo with their own call-and-response phrases

Lesson 3 – The Swing Era

Objectives

- To listen to an example of big band music from the Swing Era
- To perform different strands of the texture, both separately and together
- To improvise on a 12-bar blues using chord notes

Resources

- Pupils' worksheets on 'The Swing Era' and 'The 12-Bar Blues'
- YouTube recording of Glenn Miller's 'In the Mood': https://youtu.be/_CI-0E_jses
- Keyboards and ukuleles/guitars (if available/playable)
- Drum kit and/or some unpitched classroom percussion instruments
- Double bass or bass guitar (if available/playable)
- Piano or guitar for teacher

Procedure

Starter – listening/appraising

- Pupils listen to recording of Glenn Miller's 'In the Mood'
- Pupils write down the instruments in the Glenn Miller Band. Here are the answers:

Frontline instruments	Rhythm section
4 Saxophones	Piano
4 Trombones	Guitar
4 Trumpets	Double Bass
	Drum kit

Main – performing

- Pupils practise performing the melody and chord sequence in this piece in these different ways:
    - **Scat-singing** the tune to 'doo-bee doo-bee doo-bee doo-bee doo-bee doo-wah'
    - Playing the chord sequence, either on the beat or in a syncopated rhythm
    - Playing the bass line on the beat, either by repeating the root of each chord or with a **walking bass**
    - Playing the melody on a keyboard – it is based entirely on chord notes, starting on E
    - Improvising on the chord notes (don't forget to change the notes when the chord changes)
    - Improvising on the blues scale (see the bottom of the sheet music)
- Teacher assesses pupils on their performance (see Assessment Sheet)

Plenary – performing

- Having tried out the different ways of performing 'In the Mood', the teacher assigns different pupils to different strands of the musical texture:
    - melody – sung or played
    - chords – 12-bar blues played on keyboards, ukuleles or guitars
    - bass line – static or walking bass on keyboards, double bass or bass guitar
    - percussion – 'ten-to-ten' rhythm on ride cymbal/shakers/scrapers, drums on beat
- The whole class plays 'In the Mood', playing the different strands of the texture together

Lesson 4 – Later Jazz Styles

Objective
- To listen to some different styles of jazz after 1945: Bebop, Latin Jazz, Cool Jazz and Rock Fusion
- To become familiar with the different rhythmic 'grooves' for Swing, Latin Jazz, and Jazz-Rock

Resources
- Pupils' worksheet
- YouTube clips
    - Bebop – Charlie Parker – 'Anthropology' https://youtu.be/5pqSqwh9rfQ
    - Latin Jazz - Astrud Gilberto, João Gilberto and Stan Getz – 'The Girl from Ipanema' https://www.youtube.com/watch?v=c5QfXjsoNe4
    - Cool Jazz – Miles Davis – 'Moon Dreams' https://youtu.be/8Qq2NLrbL7o
    - Rock Fusion – Billy Taylor Trio – 'I Wish I Knew How It Would Feel to be Free' https://www.youtube.com/watch?v=6qAg9p8QpG8
- Drum Kit with drumsticks and brushes
- Maracas and claves

Procedure

Starter - Appraising
- Pupils read through the worksheet 'Later Jazz Styles'

Main - Performing
- Identify the instruments on the drum kit (bass drum, snare drum, hi-hat, tom toms, crash/ride cymbal)
- Try a basic rock rhythm on the body drum kit while siting down: slap 'hi-hat' (left thigh) on all beats 1 2 3 4; play 'bass drum' (right foot stamp with heel on ground) on beats 1 and 3; slap 'snare drum' (right thigh) on beats 2 and 4
- In groups of three, try the same rhythm on the drum kit (one pupil sits down to operate the bass drum pedal, on their left another pupil plays the snare drum on beats 2 and 4, on their left another pupil plays single beats or continuous quavers on the closed hi-hat)
- Listen to teacher playing a 'ten to ten' swing rhythm on the ride cymbal, instead of the straight quavers on the hi-hat, and playing a continuous 'brushing' sound on the snare drum
- In groups of three, try the same rhythm on the drum kit (one pupil sits down to operate the bass drum pedal, on their left another pupil plays the snare drum on beats 2 and 4, on their left another pupil plays single beats or continuous quavers on the closed hi-hat)
- Finally, try a Latin rhythm: a 3+2 clave (♩. ♩. ♩ | 𝄽 ♩ ♩ 𝄽) using a rim shot on the drum kit or the claves, with continuous quavers on the maracas

Plenary - Listening
- Pupils listen to the four YouTube clips in a random order and identify which style each one belongs to

Lesson 5 – When the Saints go Marching In

Objectives
- To demonstrate knowledge of jazz in a listening exercise
- To perform a simple jazz standard on the keyboard

Resources
- Pupils' worksheet: 'Listening Exercise' and 'When the Saints Go Marching In'
- YouTube clip: 'When the Saints Go Marching In' by Louis Armstrong (http://www.youtube.com/watch?v=5WADCJ4_KmU)
- Keyboards

Procedure

Starter – listening
- Pupils complete listening exercise on Louis Armstrong's performance of 'When the Saints Go Marching In'

Main – performing
- Watch, and listen to, demonstration of 'When the Saints Go Marching In' on piano or keyboard
- Learn to play 'When the Saints Go Marching In' on keyboard:
    - Most pupils should aim to learn the melody in the right hand
    - Less able pupils should play the chord (or just the bass line) from the boxed chord symbols
    - More able pupils go by themselves, playing the melody in the right hand and the accompanying chords in the left hand

Plenary - performance
- All pupils demonstrate their version of 'When the Saints Go Marching In' on keyboard (assessed)

Lesson 6 – Improvising Assessment

Objectives
- To demonstrate improvisation skills using 'When the Saints Go Marching In'

Resources
- Pupils' worksheets: 'When the Saints Go Marching In'
- Keyboards
- Practice rooms or breakout areas

Procedure

Starter - Listening
- Listen to teacher demonstrating improvisation techniques with 'When the Saints Go Marching In': changing rhythm, changing pitch, scat singing, etc.
- Look at

Main - Improvising
- Practise improvising 'When the Saints Go Marching In'
- Those pupils who wish to sing should go a practice room or breakout area

Plenary
- Play or sing improvisation on 'When the Saints Go Marching In' to class
- Teacher assesses improvisation using Assessment Sheet (see below)

Jazz – Assessment Sheet

CLASS __ Name	Performing *In the Mood* — Plays with sense of pulse	Plays correct chord sequence	Plays simple bass line (roots of chords)	Plays with syncopated/swing rhythms	Plays bass/melody pattern based on	Listening *When the Saints* — Identifies context (qus1-3)	Identifies melodic instruments (qu4+7)	Identifies drums (qu 5)	Identifies cymbals (qu6)	Identifies other features (qu8-10)	Improvising *When the Saints* — Improvises with sense of pulse	Improvises with different rhythms	Improvises with swing rhythms	Improvises with different pitches	Improvises with chords OR scat singing	Comments

Year 9

Dance Music
Gamelan
Minimalism
Latin Music
Romantic Music
Gospel, Blues and Soul

Dance Music

Year 9 – Michaelmas Term (September to November)

Objectives

- To differentiate between examples dance music through time, from the Renaissance pavane to present-day dubstep
- To learn to play the 'circle progression' Am-Dm-G-C-F-B dim-E in 'I Will Survive'
- To participate in a group performance of 'I Will Survive'
- To compose a club dance track using www.soundation.com

Lesson Overview

- Lesson 1: Metre
- Lesson 2: Instruments
- Lesson 3: Disco
- Lesson 4: Interim Assessment
- Lesson 5: Performing/Composing 1
- Lesson 6: Performing/Composing 2
- Lesson 7: Performing/Composing 3
- Lesson 8: Performing/Composing 4

Subject-specific vocabulary

- Periods, dances, time signatures and instrumentation:
    - Renaissance – pavane (2/2) – viols, crumhorns and side drums
    - Baroque – gigue (6/8) – oboes, trumpets, timpani, strings
    - Classical – minuet (3/4) – double woodwind, horns, trumpets, timpani, strings
    - Romantic – waltz (3/4) – double/triple woodwind, full brass, harp, strings
    - Modern – disco (4/4) – electric/bass guitars, drum kit, piano, strings
    - Contemporary – dubstep (4/4) – electronic drum machine, samplers, synths

Assessments

- Performing (keyboard) –accompaniment for 'I Will Survive'
- Composing – club dance track (Peer Assessment)
- Listening – 3 Listening exercises (Disco, Club Dance, GCSE 2011 qu6 on Moby)

Lesson 1: Metre

Objective
- To differentiate between common time signatures in performing and listening
- To associate six periods in Music History with their typical dances

Resources
- Dance Music workbooks
- YouTube videos for listening exercise (the first four all show the instruments as well):
    - 16th c. Renaissance – Susato's Pavane 'La Bataille' – https://www.youtube.com/watch?v=ts8vhusJOBo
    - 17th c. Baroque – Bach's Orchestral Suite No. 3: Gigue – https://www.youtube.com/watch?v=-k73xKG4pn8
    - 18th c. Classical – Haydn's London Symphony: Minuet – https://www.youtube.com/watch?v=aaEJ7dGZsec
    - 19th c. Romantic – Tchaikovsky's Waltz of the Flowers from the Nutcracker
    - https://www.youtube.com/watch?v=XwgOWDUlDgY
    - 20th c. Modern (Disco) – Gloria Gaynor's I Will Survive https://www.youtube.com/watch?v=ZBR2G-iI3-I
    - 21st c. Contemporary (Dubstep) - Stepcat's 'The Jitterbug EP' https://www.youtube.com/watch?v=kI7Cod-0ORs

Procedure

Starter: Listening
- Teacher distributes workbooks (one per pupil).
- Pupils listen to six excerpts of dance music, one from each of the last six centuries, but in a random order. For each excerpt, write the century (16th-21st) and the period of music history.

Main: Performing
- Learn to clap dance rhythms on front page of workbook, discussing differences in time signature.
- Discuss the increasing use of syncopation as time progresses, particularly in modern and contemporary dance music.
- Copy teacher sitting on chair and playing imaginary bass drum with right foot (heel on floor), stamping on four beats in a bar ('four-one-the-floor')
- Copy teacher continuing the 'four-one-the-floor' while clapping on the second and fourth beats of each bar. Alternatively, an imaginary snare drum can be played by slapping right thigh with left hand.
- Copy teacher continuing the 'four-one-the-floor' while tapping a variety of hi-hat rhythms on the left thigh: continuous quavers or (more difficult) off-beat quavers with the right hand only, or (more difficult) continuous semiquavers with both hands.

Plenary: Listening

- Listen to the to six excerpts of dance music again, this time in chronological order, writing the period of music history, the type of dance, and the time signature.
- Pupils who play instruments should bring them to the next lesson

Lesson 2: Instruments

Objective
- To differentiate between common time signatures while performing and listening
- To associate six periods in Music History with their typical dances

Resources
- Pupils' instruments (if applicable)
- Dance Music workbooks
- YouTube videos for listening exercise (the first four all show the instruments as well):
    - 16th c. Renaissance – Susato's Pavane 'La Bataille' – https://www.youtube.com/watch?v=ts8vhusJOBo
    - 17th c. Baroque – Bach's Orchestral Suite No. 3: Gigue – https://www.youtube.com/watch?v=-k73xKG4pn8
    - 18th c. Classical – Haydn's London Symphony: Minuet – https://www.youtube.com/watch?v=aaEJ7dGZsec
    - 19th c. Romantic – Tchaikovsky's Waltz of the Flowers from the Nutcracker
    - https://www.youtube.com/watch?v=XwgOWDUlDgY
    - 20th c. Modern (Disco) – Gloria Gaynor's I Will Survive https://www.youtube.com/watch?v=ZBR2G-iI3-I
    - 21st c. Contemporary (Dubstep) - Stepcat's 'The Jitterbug EP' https://www.youtube.com/watch?v=kI7Cod-0ORs

Procedure

Starter: Listening
- Listen to the six excerpts in chronological order and tick the instruments.
- Discuss the answers, noting how the instrumental groups become larger until the Romantic period. Electric instruments emerge in the modern period, while the contemporary dubstep is completely electronic (albeit using samples of instruments such as the clarinet):
    - Renaissance – pavane (2/2) – viols, crumhorns and side drums
    - Baroque – gigue (6/8) – oboes, trumpets, timpani, strings
    - Classical – minuet (3/4) – double woodwind, horns, trumpets, timpani, strings
    - Romantic – waltz (3/4) – double/triple woodwind, full brass, harp, strings
    - Modern – disco (4/4) – electric/bass guitars, drum kit, piano, strings
    - Contemporary – dubstep (4/4) – electronic drum machine, samplers, synths

Main: Performing
- Assign parts and rehearse classroom performance of Susato's Pavane 'La Bataille'

Plenary: Performing
- Perform and record classroom performance of Susato's Pavane 'La Bataille'
- Listen to and discuss recording

Lesson 3: Disco

Objectives
- To discover the musical features of Disco music
- To learn the melody and chord sequence for the disco song 'I Will Survive'

Resources
- Dance music workbook: pages 4-5 (Disco/I Will Survive)
- YouTube videos for listening exercise:
    - Gloria Gaynor's 'I Will Survive': https://www.youtube.com/watch?v=ZBR2G-iI3-I
    - Bee Gees' 'Staying Alive': https://www.youtube.com/watch?v=Fa9n7GirhsI
    - Rose Royce's 'Car Wash': https://www.youtube.com/watch?v=GFVcqVM9vhw
- Keyboards and headphones

Procedure

Starter: Listening
- Listen to the three Disco songs and answer the questions on worksheet:

    1. How many beats in a bar are there? 4
    2. Roughly how many beats per minute (bpm) are there? 120
    3. Which high plucked string instrument is playing? Electric guitar
    4. Which low plucked string instrument is playing? (Electric) bass (guitar)
    5. Which high bowed string instrument is playing? Violin
    6. Which low-pitched drum in the drum kit plays on all of these beats? Bass drum
    7. Which higher-pitched drum in the drum kit plays on the 2nd and 4th beats? Snare drum
    8. Which cymbal in the drum kit plays on the offbeat quavers (half-beat notes)? Hi-hat

Main: Performing
- Distribute worksheets (one per pupil) and learn to sing, phrase by phrase, 'I Will Survive' from sheet music; perform the song as a class
- 'I Will Survive' is based on a chord sequence known as a 'circle' progression (because it comes full circle). the worksheet, complete the notes and diagrams for the chords Am, Dm, G, C, F, B dim and E
- As a class, play the 'circle' progression from the worksheet: Am-Dm-G-C-F-B dim-E-E
- In pairs on keyboards, learn to play the 'circle' progression with the right hand, keeping a steady sense of the four beats in each bar. This task can be differentiated as follows:
    - Less able pupils only play the bass line (i.e. the first note/root of each chord)
    - more able pupils have a keyboard to themselves and play with both hands

Plenary: Performing (keyboard)

- Some or all pupils play their work-in-progress to the rest of the class (try to show the range of differentiated tasks above)
- During next lesson, all pupils will be assessed on:
    - Performing on the keyboard
    - Listening to the six dances/periods studied

Lesson 4: Interim Assessment

Objectives

- To demonstrate understanding of the six dances/periods studied
- To perform the 'circle progression' on the keyboard

Resources

- Pupil's workbook
- YouTube links for six dances (see Lesson 1)
- Keyboards and headphones

Procedure

Starter – listening

- Pupils complete Listening Assessment on back of workbook (page 12) – workbooks must not be opened during assessment
- Pupils listen to the six dances in a random order and identify the following for each one:
    - Century [1]
    - Period of Music History [1]
    - Name of dance [1]
    - Time Signature [1]
    - Three instruments [3]

Main – Performing

- Pupils demonstrates the 'circle' progression (as used in 'I Will Survive'), differentiated as follows:
    - Less able pupils only play the bass line (i.e. the first note/root of each chord)
    - more able pupils have a keyboard to themselves and play with both hands
- Pupils practise the 'circle' progression, differentiated as above.
- Any pupils who do not wish to perform in front of the class should be assessed before the plenary.

Plenary – Performing

- Pupils perform 'circle' progression to the rest of the class, assessed by teacher.
- Pupils should bring their instruments next lesson if they would like to play them in a group performance of 'I Will Survive'.

The listening and performing assessments form the basis of the October grades.

Lessons 5: Performing/Composing

Each of the performing and composing projects contributes 30% towards the November exam.

Objectives

- To participate in a group performance of 'I Will Survive'
- To compose a club dance track using www.soundation.com

Resources

- Dance workbook
- Practice rooms
- Instruments as necessary (see below)
- Laptops with access to www.soundation.com (sequencing website)

Procedure

Starter - Performing

- The class is divided into groups of 4-6, made up as follows:
  - One or two pupils (depending on their confidence and ability) singing the melody
  - Two pupils (or one more able pupil) play the 'circle' progression on the keyboard :
    - One (less able) pupil plays the bass line A-D-G-C-F-B-E-E
    - One pupil plays the chord sequence Am-Dm-G-C-F-B dim-E-E
  - Between one and three pupils sharing the drum kit rhythm, depending on ability:
    - One pupil plays the 'four-one-the-floor' beat on a tom tom (doubling for bass drum with a large, soft beater
    - One pupil plays the snare drum on the second and fourth beats of the bar
    - One pupil plays the hi-hat rhythm (continuous quavers, offbeat quavers or continuous semiquavers)
  - One or more pupils playing the bass line on their own instrument (e.g. cello)

Main – Performing

- The groups go to practice rooms and other breakout areas to practise 'I Will Survive', monitored by the teacher.

Plenary – Composing

Teacher goes through composing project.

Teacher explains that the pupils have three or four more lessons to complete both projects before the exams.

Roughly half the class practise their performance in groups while the other half compose individually; swap halfway through the lesson.

Lessons 6-8: Performing/Composing

Objectives
- To participate in a group performance of 'I Will Survive'
- To compose a club dance track using www.soundation.com

Resources
- Dance workbook
- Practice rooms
- Instruments as necessary (see below)
- Laptops with access to www.soundation.com (sequencing website)

Procedure
Roughly half the class practise their performance in groups while the other half compose individually; swap halfway through the lesson.

Composing
- Teacher demonstrates how to complete Sessioneof the composing task using www.soundation.com (sequencing website)
- Main - performing
- Using laptop, pupils compose their drum rhythm

Performing
- The groups practise 'I Will Survive' as follows:
    - One or two pupils (depending on their confidence and ability) singing the melody
    - Two pupils (or one more able pupil) play the 'circle' progression on the keyboard :
        - One (less able) pupil plays the bass line A-D-G-C-F-B-E-E
        - One pupil plays the chord sequence Am-Dm-G-C-F-B dim-E-E
    - Between one and three pupils sharing the drum kit rhythm, depending on ability:
        - One pupil plays the 'four-one-the-floor' beat on a tom tom (doubling for bass drum with a large, soft beater
        - One pupil plays the snare drum on the second and fourth beats of the bar
        - One pupil plays the hi-hat rhythm (continuous quavers, offbeat quavers or continuous semiquavers)
    - One or more pupils playing the bass line on their own instrument (e.g. cello)

Gamelan

Year 9 – Michaelmas Term (November to December)

Objectives

- To learn about the instruments of the Indonesian gamelan
- To learn how to play interlocking patterns within a gamelan
- To compose a heterophonic piece for the gamelan

Lesson Overview

- Lesson 1: Introducing the Gamelan
- Lesson 2: Performing gamelan music
- Lesson 3: Extending the performance *(optional)*
- Lesson 4: Composing for the gamelan
- Lesson 5: Performing and evaluating compositions

Subject-specific vocabulary

- Metallophones: demung (large), saron (medium) and peking (small)
- Gongs: ageng (large), kempul (medium) and kenong (small)
- Other percussion: ciblon (double-headed drum) and chengcheng (finger cymbals)
- Structure: buka (introduction), balungan (main melody) and suwuk (ending)
- Texture: interlocking patterns, heterophony

Assessments

- Performing (whole class gamelan) – 'Lancaran Bintang' (traditional)
- Composing - rehearsing and leading whole class ensemble in playing gamelan piece
- Listening – traditional gamelan piece 'Ima Ima'

Lesson 1: Introducing the Gamelan

Resources

- YouTube video of Balinese gamelan: https://www.youtube.com/watch?v=Ti9fajX4PF8
- 4-sided worksheet on Gamelan (Gamelan/Instruments/Layout/Lancaran Bintang)
- School gamelan (9 metallophones, 3 gongs, up to 12 finger cymbals, drum)

Procedure

Starter: Listening

- Watch and listen to YouTube video of Balinese gamelan

- Quick oral questions:
    - Where is this music from? (South East Asia/Indonesia/Bali.)
    - What is it called? (Gamelan)

Main: Appraising

- As a class, read through first two pages of worksheet: 'Gamelan' and 'Gamelan instruments'.

- Label the instruments on page 3 of the worksheet ('Layout of the Gamelan'), then set out the classroom in the same pattern.

- On page 4 of the worksheet ('Lancaran Bintang'), fill in the names and, where prompted, the missing musical patterns for the instruments.

Plenary: Performing

- Try out each part, one at a time (do not attempt to combine the parts at this stage). Those pupils playing metallophones can try one four-beat section at a time, rather than the whole 16-beat cycle. Pupils rotate around the instruments so that they can try different instruments and find their level.

Lesson 2: Performing Gamelan Music

Resources

- Recording of 'Lancaran Bintang'
  https://drive.google.com/file/d/0BzpskpY1cquLRjU2d2N5S2lZcVE/edit?usp=sharing

- 4-sided worksheet on Gamelan from last lesson

- Single-sided 'Gamelan: self-evaluation' sheet

- School gamelan (9 metallophones, 3 gongs, up to 12 finger cymbals, drum)

Procedure

Starter: Listening

- Listen to recording of 'Lancaran Bintang' with worksheet

- Recap the instruments of the gamelan and what they play in the piece

Main: Performing

- Set up the gamelan according to page 3 of the worksheet ('The Layout of the Gamelan')
- Build up the performance one part at a time and breaking the 16-beat cycle into 4-beat sections where necessary.

- Combine groups of similar instruments (gongs, metallophones and unpitched percussion) before attempting to put together the whole gamelan.

- Pupils should try out <u>as many different instruments as they wish</u> to find their level. Eventually the performance task should be differentiated as follows (from the least able to the most able pupils):

  1. Gong ageng and ciblon
  2. Chengcheng, gong kempul and kenong
  3. Demung
  4. Saron
  5. Peking

Plenary: Appraising

Each pupil evaluates their own performance by completing the self-evaluation sheet.

Lesson 3: Extending the performance *(optional)*

This lesson should only be taught when there is enough time to teach all five lessons in this project.

Resources

- Recording of 'Lancaran Bintang'
  https://drive.google.com/file/d/0BzpskpY1cquLRjU2d2N5S2lZcVE/edit?usp=sharing

- Single-sided 'Lancaran Bintang – full score' sheet

- School gamelan (9 metallophones, 3 gongs, up to 12 finger cymbals, drum)

- Digital recording device

Procedure

Starter: Listening

- Listen to recording of 'Lancaran Bintang' again, this time with full score

- Quick oral question: how is this version different from the version we played last lesson?
  - It has an introduction (buka) and an ending (suwuk)
  - The main melody (balungan) is played several times
  - The tempo speeds up and slows down in the middle of the piece
  - (More advanced) the metallophones come in one-by-one in the main section, thus creating a variety of texture

Main: Performing

- Set up the gamelan according to page 3 of the worksheet ('The Layout of the Gamelan')
- Recap on main section and practise until it is secure. (It is probably best by this stage to encourage pupils to 'specialise' in instruments, according to ability, as detailed below (from the least able to the most able pupils):

  1. Gong ageng and ciblon
  2. Chengcheng, gong kempul and kenong
  3. Demung
  4. Saron
  5. Peking

- Practise the introduction and ending one part at a time, then put together

Plenary: Performing and Appraising

- Perform and record the whole piece.

- Listen to the recording and discuss.

Lesson 4: Composing for the gamelan

Resources

- Single-sided worksheet 'Composing Gamelan Music'
- 6 small and medium metallophones (pekings and sarons) from gamelan set
- 6 pairs of finger cymbals (chengchengs) from gamelan set
- Single-sided worksheet 'Gamelan Listening Exercise'
- Recording of 'Ima Ima'
  https://drive.google.com/file/d/0BzpskpY1cquLdnFQaFBmMmJRRms/edit?usp=sharing

Procedure

Starter - Composing

- Teacher distributes worksheets entitled 'Composing Gamelan Music' and goes through it, explaining the composing process and assessment criteria

Main – Composing

- Pupils go into pairs (if there is an odd number, a more confident/able pupil can go by themselves), go to a practice room or other area and compose their own Lancaran (16-beat cycle). Pupils should take a saron or peking to help you compose the melody and chengcheng to work out the rhythms.
- Teacher goes around all of the practice areas to check progress and assist pupils

Plenary – Listening

- Pupils complete 'Gamelan Listening Exercise' (assessed by teacher)

N.B. Before the next lesson, the teacher should mark both the 'Gamelan Listening Exercise' and the written element of the 'Composing Gamelan Music' worksheets.

Lesson 5: Performing and evaluating compositions

Resources

- Photocopied and stapled booklet for each pupil containing all the 'Composing Gamelan Music' worksheets

- School gamelan (9 metallophones, 3 gongs, up to 12 finger cymbals, drum)

- Christmas song(s), e.g. Jingle Bell Rock

Procedure

Starter – Composing

- Pupils and teacher set up the gamelan as before

Main – Composing

- Each pair of pupils who composed together last lesson have five minutes to lead the rest of the class in realising their composition.

- The composers are responsible for leading both the rehearsal and the performance of their joint piece. They decide which of their classmates play which instruments and then should direct them to play their composition the way it was intended.

- The teacher assesses how the each of the pupils realises their gamelan compositions.

Plenary – Performing

- If there is time, perform one or more Christmas songs as a class.

Minimalism

Objectives
- To experience, through listening and performing, how a whole piece music can be created from one simple idea
- To practise minimalist techniques through performing and composing
- To listen to and analyse music by the minimalist composers John Adams, Steve Reich, Philip Glass, Michael Nyman and Terry Riley

Lesson Overview
- Lesson 1 – Motif and Ostinato
- Lesson 2 – Note Addition and Note Subtraction
- Lesson 3 – Canon and Layering
- Lesson 4 – Augmentation and Diminution
- Lesson 5 – Phasing and Phase-Shifting
- Lesson 6 – Class Composition/Performance 'in C'

Subject-specific vocabulary
- **MINIMALISM** – a style of music which started in the USA in the 1960s. It is characterised by simple, repetitive patterns which are transformed throughout the piece, using various techniques, including:
    - **Motif** – a basic rhythmic or melodic pattern
    - **Ostinato** – a repeating pattern
    - **Note Addition** – gradually adding notes to a motif
    - **Note Subtraction** – gradually taking away notes from a motif
    - **Canon** – two or more parts performing the same motif but starting at different times
    - **Layering** – the process of adding or taking away parts (or layers)
    - **Augmentation** – the motif played in longer note values
    - **Diminution** – the motif played in shorter note values
    - **Phasing** – two or more parts gradually getting 'out of sync' with each other
    - **Phase-shifting** – two or more parts getting 'out of sync' by one beat at a time

Assessments
- **Performing** – Steve Reich's *Clapping Music*
- **Composing** – minimalist piece for two instruments, based on a simple one-bar motif
- **Listening** – listening exercise on Steve Reich's *Electric Counterpoint*

Lesson 1 – Motif and Ostinato

Objectives
- To learn about Motif and Ostinato by listening to John Adams' *A Short Ride in a Fast Machine*
- To compose a motif and to perform it as an ostinato

Resources
- YouTube clip of John Adams' *A Short Ride in a Fast Machine*
  https://www.youtube.com/watch?v=T1x2x1nSsE4
- A mixture of pitched and unpitched percussion instruments (enough for one per pupil)

Procedure

Starter – Listening
- Listen to the first 1 minutes and 50 seconds of John Adams' *A Short Ride in a Fast Machine*
- Are there any repeating patterns in the music? (Yes.)
- Teacher explains that each basic pattern is called a **MOTIF** and a repeating pattern is called an **OSTINATO**
- Are the patterns in this music simple or complicated? (Simple.)
- Teacher explains that this style of music, using simple, repetitive patterns, is known as **MINIMALISM** which started in the USA in the 1960s.

Main – Composing
- Distribute pitched and unpitched percussion instruments (enough for one per pupil) – differentiate so that more able pupils are playing pitched percussion instruments
- Teacher makes up an example motif for pupils to copy, but they keep repeating it (so it becomes an ostinato)
- Some (or all) pupils make up their own example motif for other pupils to copy as an ostinato
- Teacher and pupils with a pitched percussion instrument play a simple pentatonic motif; pupils with an unpitched percussion instrument imitate only the rhythm
- Pupils with an unpitched percussion instrument play a rhythm which those with a pitched percussion instrument imitate on one note
- Pupils go into pairs to compose a one-bar motif on their instruments (or on sequencing/notation software, if preferred by the teacher)

Plenary – Performing
- Pairs of pupils play their one-bar motif, repeated as an ostinato, to the rest of the class, either on their instruments or on the computer

Lesson 2 – Note Addition and Note Subtraction

Objective

- To learn about Note Addition and Note Subtraction by listening to part of Philip Glass' *Einstein on the Beach*
- To apply this learning to composition/performance of minimalist piece

Resources

- Philip Glass' *Einstein on the Beach*, Act I Scene 2 'Trial'
  https://www.youtube.com/watch?v=ZOvlPvXXggs&t=1m11s

Procedure

Starter – Listening

- Listen to Philip Glass' *Einstein on the Beach*, Act I Scene 2 'Trial' Concentrate on the motif in the solo violin part, which changes gradually over time. What happens in the first half of the extract? (More notes are added.) What happens in the second half? (Notes are taken away.)
- These techniques are known as **Note Addition** and **Note Subtraction**.

Main – Composing

- Teacher asks for a volunteer pair of pupils to demonstrate the process described below
- In the same pairs as last week, and using the same method (live performance or computer), pupils create:
  - an introduction to their piece using **Note Addition**, starting with one note and adding one note at a time until it becomes the whole motif (composed last week), and
  - an ending to their piece using **Note Subtraction**, starting with the whole motif and taking away one note at a time until there is only one note left

Plenary – Performing

- Pairs of pupils play their work-in-progress to the rest of the class, either on their instruments or on the computer, structuring the piece as follows:
  1. Introduction – **NOTE ADDITION** – starting with one note and adding one note at a time until it becomes the whole motif
  2. Middle section – motif performed several times as an ostinato
  3. Ending – **NOTE SUBTRACTION** – starting with the whole motif and taking away one note at a time until there is only one note left

Lesson 3 – Canon and Layering

Objective

- To learn about **CANON** and **LAYERING** by listening to Steve Reich's *Electric Counterpoint*
- To demonstrate knowledge and recognition of the following features in an assessed listening exercise:
    1. **Motif** (or 'cell') – a basic rhythmic or melodic pattern
    2. **Ostinato** – a repeating pattern
    3. **Note Addition** – gradually adding notes to a motif
    4. **Canon** – two or more parts performing the same motif but starting at different times
    5. **Layering** – the process of adding or taking away parts (or layers)
- To integrate **CANON** and **LAYERING** into pupils' own compositions

Resources

- YouTube clip of 3rd Movement (fast) from *Electric Counterpoint* by Steve Reich (with score): https://www.youtube.com/watch?v=_TKVpUSWCug
- Five listening questions on presentation slide or worksheet

Procedure

Starter - Listening

- Listen to the first minute and a half of 3rd Movement (fast) from *Electric Counterpoint*
- Teacher explains the techniques of **LAYERING** (where the parts come in one at a time) and **CANON** (where the parts play the same motif but starting at different times)
- Listen two more times to the piece, answering these five questions:
    1. What is the name of the one-bar pattern played at the beginning? MOTIF
    2. What word describes the way it keeps repeating? OSTINATO
    3. What technique is used by the next instrument to build up to the full pattern? NOTE ADDITION
    4. The first five instruments come in one at a time. What is this technique called? LAYERING
    5. The first five instruments to be heard all play the same pattern, but starting at different times. What is this technique called? CANON

Main – Composing

- Teacher asks for a volunteer pair of pupils to demonstrate the process described below
- In the same pairs as last week, and using the same method (live performance or computer), pupils create:
    - **LAYERING**: A section of the piece where one of the two parts/layers is added and/or taken away
    - **CANON**: A section of the piece where one of the parts starts the ostinato at a different time (i.e. different beat of the bar) from the other part

Plenary – Performing

- Pairs of pupils play their work-in-progress to the rest of the class, either on their instruments or on the computer, structuring the piece as follows:
    1. Introduction – **NOTE ADDITION** – starting with one note and adding one note at a time until it becomes the whole motif
    2. Middle section – containing the following subsections, in any order
        - **OSTINATO**: motif performed several times
        - **LAYERING**: A section of the piece where one of the two parts/layers is added and/or taken away
        - **CANON**: A section of the piece where one of the parts starts the ostinato at a different time (i.e. different beat of the bar) from the other part
    3. Ending – **NOTE SUBTRACTION** – starting with the whole motif and taking away one note at a time until there is only one note left

Lesson 4 – Augmentation and Diminution

Objective
- To learn Augmentation and Diminution by listening to part of Michael Nyman's *The Piano*
- To apply this learning to composition/performance of minimalist piece

Resources
- YouTube recording of the traditional Scottish folk melody 'The Flowers o' the Forest': https://www.youtube.com/watch?v=D8ebu8warnk
- YouTube recording of the 'Silver-fingered fling' (from *The Piano*) by Michael Nyman: https://www.youtube.com/watch?v=efMOqnTdboU

Procedure

Starter – Listening
- Listen to recording of the traditional Scottish folk melody 'The Flowers o' the Forest'
- Now listen to recording of the 'Silver-fingered fling' (from *The Piano*) by Michael Nyman, which uses the melody (tune) from 'The Flowers o' the Forest'
- What happens in the first half of the extract? (The melody is played slowly/the note-lengths are doubled.) What happens in the second half? (The melody is played quickly/the note-lengths are halved.)
- These techniques are known as **AUGMENTATION** and **DIMINUTION**.

Main – Composing
- Teacher asks for a volunteer pair of pupils to demonstrate the process described below
- In the same pairs as last week, and using the same method (live performance or computer), pupils create:
  - A transformation of their motif using **AUGMENTATION** – where the note-lengths are doubled
  - A transformation of their motif using **DIMINUTION** – where the note-lengths are halved
  - More advanced pupils should try to compose/perform the transformed motif(s) at the same time as the ostinato with the original note-lengths

Plenary – Performing

- Pairs of pupils play their final composition to the rest of the class, either on their instruments or on the computer, structuring the piece as follows:
    1. Introduction – **NOTE ADDITION** – starting with one note and adding one note at a time until it becomes the whole motif
    2. Middle section – containing the following subsections, in any order
        - **OSTINATO**: motif performed several times
        - **LAYERING**: A section of the piece where one of the two parts/layers is added and/or taken away
        - **CANON**: A section of the piece where one of the parts starts the ostinato at a different time (i.e. different beat of the bar) from the other part
        - **AUGMENTATION** – where the note-lengths are doubled
        - **DIMINUTION** – where the note-lengths are halved
    3. Ending – **NOTE SUBTRACTION** – starting with the whole motif and taking away one note at a time until there is only one note left
- Teacher assesses compositions according to the following criteria:
    - Effective opening using note addition
    - Uses a repeated motif as an ostinato
    - Uses a canon and/or layering
    - Uses augmentation and/or diminution
    - Effective ending using note subtraction
- Alternatively, the composition can be further extended by the use of **PHASE-SHIFTING** – see next lesson plan

Lesson 5 – Phasing and Phase-Shifting

Objective

- To understand two **minimalist** techniques, **phasing** and **phase-shifting**, by listening to Steve Reich's *Drumming* and *Clapping Music*

Resources

- YouTube video Steve Reich 'Drumming' - Portland Percussion Group https://www.youtube.com/watch?v=doJk4yPwJDk (from 0.00 to 2.20)
- YouTube video 'Steve Reich - Clapping Music (Scrolling)' https://www.youtube.com/watch?v=lzkOFJMI5i8
- Single-sided worksheet with blank grid for notating Steve Reich's *Clapping Music*

Procedure

Starter - Listening

- Watch and listen to Steve Reich's 'Drumming'. What happens to the ostinato on the two drums towards the end of the extract? (It goes out of sync/out of phase.)
- Teacher explains that this process is known as **PHASING**. Now here is a similar, but not the same, process.
- Watch animated score of Steve Reich's *Clapping Music*. Can you describe what is happening in the music?
- Discuss how the whole piece is based on a clapping pattern, performed in two ways simultaneously:
    - **OSTINATO** (repeating same pattern)
    - **PHASE-SHIFTING** (pattern 'shifts' one beat ahead to go out of 'phase' with the repeating pattern)

Main - Performing

- Practise clapping the ostinato by copying the teacher
- Write down the pattern on row 1 of the worksheet by listening to the teacher clap the ostinato slowly whilst counting the beats 1-12; check the answer against the version on the board, correcting if necessary
- Teacher gives any pupils struggling at this stage Worksheet B (where they only complete half the pattern)
- Complete the performing score of Clapping Music on 12x12 grid by shifting the pattern one box to the left on each subsequent row. The box that 'falls off' the left side of the grid is added to the right side
- As a class, practise performing the phase-shifting rhythm slowly and counting the beats out loud
- Split the class into two groups and perform the piece with one group clapping the ostinato and the other clapping the phase-shifting rhythm
- Swap the groups around so they are doing the 'other' rhythm (ostinato or phase-shifting)
- In pairs, pupils practise 'Clapping Music'

Plenary - Performing

- Perform Clapping Music in pairs – assessed by teacher giving up to five marks as follows:
    - Shows clear sense of pulse
    - Shows awareness of ensemble
    - Claps basic rhythm correctly
    - Maintains independent part (ostinato or phase-shifting) within ensemble
    - Creates several different cross-rhythms as a pair (i.e. effective phase-shifting is achieved through three or more cycles, whether the pupil being assessed is clapping ostinato or phase-shifting)

OR Main – Composing

- Pupils integrate phase-shifting into their composition

Plenary – Performing

- Pupils perform final composition in pairs

Lesson 6: Class Composition/Performance 'in C'

Objective
- To create a class minimalist composition and performance inspired by Terry Riley's 'in C'

Resources
- YouTube video of Terry Riley's 'in C' (with score)
  https://www.youtube.com/watch?v=yNi0bukYRnA
- Any mixture of pitched instruments (one per pupil)

Procedure

Starter - Listening

- Listen to the first two minutes of Terry Riley's 'in C' with the score. What keeps the ensemble together? (There is a constant pulse on a single note – high C.) Discuss how the motifs in the score are played. (The musicians play the motifs in order and but progress to the next motif at different times.)
- Teacher explains that Terry Riley's 'in C' is one of the first minimalist pieces, dating back to 1964. It is for 'any number of any kind of instruments'. There are 53 motifs, to be played in order as ostinati and in strict time with the pulse. Each player moves on to the next motif when (s)he wants to, although they should stay within 2 or 3 patterns of one another. The performance ends when everybody reaches the last motif.
- Teacher announces that the class is now going to compose and perform their own piece inspired by Terry Riley's 'in C'.

Main - Composing

- Each pupil chooses a pitched instrument (mallet instruments such as xylophones and marimbas work particularly well in this piece)
- Each pupil composes a motif on their instrument. Like Terry Riley's motifs, each motif should be 'in C', so should centre on the note and/or chord of C, with optional adjacent notes (i.e. passing, auxiliary or grace notes)
- Each pupil (with the teacher's help, if necessary) notates their motif on the board
- The teacher numbers the motifs in rough approximate order of complexity, from the simplest motif to the most complicated.
- Each motif is demonstrated by its composer and the class imitates. The performers practise each motif in turn and in unison to make sure that everyone is playing correctly and in time with the pulse
- (Optional – if desired and/or necessary) One or two pupils is/are assigned the task of keeping a steady pulse on a high C on piano or mallet instrument

Plenary - Performing

- Perform (and optionally record) the class's own composition inspired by 'in C', following these guidelines:
    - Keep in time with the pulse

- Start playing the first motif at different times (layering and canon)
- Play each motif several times in order to hear and enjoy the interlocking patterns with the other performers
- Each player moves on to the next motif when (s)he wants to, although they should stay within 2 or 3 patterns of one another
- The performance ends when everybody has played the final motif in unison a few times

Minimalism: Assessment Sheet

CLASS __	Performing — *Clapping Music*					Listening — *Electric C'point*					Composing — *Minimalist duet*					Comments
Name	Shows clear sense of pulse	Shows awareness of ensemble	Claps basic rhythm correctly	Maintains independent part in	Creates several different cross-rhythms	Identifies instruments (qus1,2)	Identifies motif/ostinato (qus3,4)	Describes rhythm (qus5,6)	Recognises note addition (qus7,8)	Identifies canon/layering (qus9,10)	Effective opening using note addition	Uses a repeated motif as an ostinato	Uses canon and/or layering	Uses augmentation and/or diminution	Effective ending using note subtraction	

164

Latin Music

KS3 Scheme of Work (6 lessons)

Objectives

- To perform a samba rhythm on unpitched percussion
- To perform the tango 'Por Una Cabeza' on unpitched percussion or keyboards (rhythm only, bass line or chords, depending on ability)
- To listen to a variety of sambas and tango
- To compose a tango using a descending bass line with a 'habanera' rhythm, chords and melody

Lesson overview

- Lesson 1 – Listening to Samba
- Lesson 2 – Performing a Samba
- Lesson 3 – Listening to Tangos
- Lesson 4 – Performing a Tango
- Lesson 5 – Composing a Tango: chords and bass line
- Lesson 6 – Composing a Tango: melody

Subject-specific vocabulary

- Samba instruments:
    - Tamborim
    - Caixa de Guerra ('War Box')
    - Cuíca
    - Repinique
    - Chocalho
    - Surdo (bass drum)
- Tango instruments: *bandoneón*, violin, piano and bass
- Habañera (dotted) rhythm
- First inversion chords
- Descending bass line
- Perfect cadence

Assessments

- Listening: Listening to Samba (Lesson 1)
- Performing: Samba band (Lesson 2, self-assessment) and 'Por Una Cabeza' (Lesson 4)
- Composing: Tango (Lesson 6)

Lesson 1 – Listening to Samba

Objectives
- To listen to the different unpitched percussion instruments, in the layers that form the texture of a samba band
- To practise clapping samba rhythms in preparation for next lesson's samba band

Resources
- Pupils' worksheets: 'Listening to Samba' and 'Performing a Samba'
- YouTube clips:
    - Raw Video: Samba Spectacle at Rio's Carnival https://youtu.be/kgFjSp5as2g
    - Empress of Carnival ("Demo of Drumming Instruments") https://youtu.be/Adw8u6gL2HE

Procedure

Starter (listening)
- Pupils watch the YouTube clip 'Raw Video: Samba Spectacle at Rio's Carnival' and answer the following questions:
    - Where is it? (Rio de Janiero, the capital Brazil).
    - What kind of music is it (samba, music for dancing).

Main (listening)
- Pupils watch YouTube clip 'Empress of Carnival ("Demo of Drumming Instruments")'
- Teacher asks pupils: what instruments were in the samba band?
- Pupils watch the video again, matching the order of instruments to the names and pictures on the worksheet 'Listening to Samba' – here are the answers:

Order	Name of instrument	Picture (A-F)	Comments
1st	Bass drum	E	Gives the first beat
2nd	Bass drum	E	Gives the second beat
3rd	Bass drum	E	Syncopated
4th	War box	C	A snare drum
5th	Repinique	A	Restarts the section
6th	Cuíca	B	Hardest to play
7th	Chocalho	F	Played by women
8th	Tambourine	D	Highest pitch

- Teacher records instruments identified on the Assessment Sheet

Plenary (performing)

- Pupils read the rhythms on the worksheet 'Performing a Samba'
- With the teacher's guidance, the pupils clap each rhythm in unison
- If they can, the pupils should practise these rhythms for next lesson

Lesson 2 – Performing a Samba

Objectives

- To perform a variety of samba rhythms, including several syncopated ones, on unpitched percussion instruments
- To evaluate own performance

Resources

- Pupils' worksheets: 'Performing a Samba'
- A variety of unpitched percussion instruments, preferably 2/3 of the following:
    - snare drums
    - tom toms
    - tambours
    - woodblocks
    - sleigh bells
- Recording device

Procedure

Starter (performing)

- Pupils clap through the rhythms on the worksheet 'Performing a Samba' in unison
- Pupils decide which rhythm(s) they are capable of playing
- The pupils divide in six groups of roughly equal size, each group focussing on a single rhythm that the pupils feel confident in playing

Main (performing)

- Each group of pupils plays through its rhythm several times
- The groups combine to create a group samba piece
- The pupils decide how to start and stop the performance and which order the different layers should be added to/taken away from the texture
- (If there is time) record and listen and evaluate group performance

Plenary (appraising)

- Pupils put instruments away and complete self-evaluation at the bottom of the worksheet 'Performing a Samba'

Lesson 3 - Listening to Tangos

Objective

- To listen to three tangos, noting their musical features (minor tonality, descending bass line, melodic sequence, alternation of root position/first inversion chords)

Resources

- YouTube clip of Carlos Gardel's 'Por Una Cabeza':
  https://www.youtube.com/watch?v=ZgcqijaUxdg
- Pupils' worksheet 'Tango'
- Piano or guitar for teacher

Procedure

Starter (listening)

- Pupils listen to Carlos Gardel's 'Por Una Cabeza'
- (For the teacher's information, this has been used in the films *Schindler's List*, *Scent of a Woman* and *True Lies*, but these are all adult films which the pupils may not have seen.)
- Pupils give their responses to the music. Dispel the myth that this is 'posh' music, as it originated in the slums of Buenos Aires!

Main (listening/appraising)

- Find out more about the background to the tango by reading the worksheet 'Tango'
- Listen to three tangos:
  - 'Por Una Cabeza' by Carlos Gardel (again)
  - 'La Cumparsita' by Gerardo Matos Rodríguez
  - 'Tango Argentino' by Matyas Sieber
- Teacher discusses/explains the musical features of a tango:
  - Four beats in a bar
  - The 'Habañera' rhythm in the bass line – see notation:
  - Dotted, syncopated, and strongly accented rhythms in the melody
  - Minor key
  - Descending bass line (by alternating of root position/first inversion chords)
  - Melodic sequences
  - Instruments in band: *bandoneón*, violin, piano and bass
  - A decisive ending using a perfect cadence ('Olé!')

Plenary (performing)

- Pupils learn to sing the melody of 'Por una Cabeza' to the English words
- Pupils learn to sing the bass line to the word 'Habañera'
- The class splits into two: one group sings the melody while the other one sings the bass line, accompanied by the teacher on the guitar or piano
- The groups swap around

169

Lesson 4 – Performing a Tango

Objective

- To perform a tango, noting its salient features (minor tonality, descending bass line, melodic sequence, alternation of root position/first inversion chords)

Resources

- Pupils' worksheet 'Performing a Tango'
- Voices or instruments suitable for melody (flute, violin, piano, keyboard)
- Instruments suitable for chords (piano, keyboard, ukulele, guitar)
- Instruments suitable for bass line (piano, keyboard, cello, double bass, bass guitar)
- Unpitched percussion instruments suitable for rhythm (claves, maracas, tambour)

Procedure

Starter (performing)

- The pupils, with the teacher's guidance, decide which part of the texture they are best suited for, depending on their ability and which instrument they have
- They should choose one of the following, in descending order of difficulty:
    - Singing or playing the melody while accompanying themselves with chords/bass line
    - singing or playing the melody (flute, violin, piano, keyboard)
    - playing the chords from the boxed chord symbols (piano, keyboard, ukulele, guitar)
    - playing the bass line from the bass clef notation or from the boxed chord symbols – use the root of the chord in root position, or the note after the forward slash if the chord is in first inversion (piano, keyboard, cello, double bass, bass guitar)
    - playing the 'Habañera' rhythm on an unpitched percussion instrument

Main (performing)

- Teacher divides the class into groups of 4-6, each group containing a variety of parts within the texture (melody, chords, bass line, rhythmic accompaniment)
- Pupils practise playing or singing 'Por una Cabeza' with the rest of the group. The pupils should tackle the piece in the following stages until they find their level:

Plenary

- Pupils perform their tangos to the rest of the class.

Lesson 5 – Composing a Tango: chords and bass line

Objective
- To compose the chord sequence and bass line for a tango, written for the piano

Resources
- Carlos Gardel's 'Por Una Cabeza': https://www.youtube.com/watch?v=ZgcqijaUxdg
- Pupils' worksheets:
    - 'Tango' (from earlier lesson)
    - 'Por una Cabeza' (from earlier lesson)
    - 'Composing a Tango' (three pages)
- Sibelius notation software OR manuscript paper

Procedure

Starter - appraising
- Listen again to 'Por Una Cabeza', reading music notation from 'Por una Cabeza' worksheet
- Recap the features of the tango on 'Tango' worksheet

Main - composing
- Compose chord sequence in A minor (more able pupils should use first inversions as well as root position chords)
- Try out different chords on the keyboard and then write the chord sequence in the grid on the worksheet
- Transfer bass line and chord sequence onto piano part on Sibelius/manuscript paper

Plenary - listening
- Class listens to some pupils' work-in-progress

Lesson 6 – Composing a Tango: melody

Objective

- To compose the melody for a tango for a solo instrument, combining with the piano accompaniment composed last lesson

Resources

- Pupils' worksheets:
    - 'Tango' (from earlier lesson)
    - 'Por una Cabeza' (from earlier lesson)
    - 'Composing a Tango' (three pages)
- Sibelius notation software OR manuscript paper

Procedure

Starter - appraising

- Teacher explains how to compose:
    - a rhythm for a motif
    - a melody for the motif
    - a development of this motif
- This is further explained on steps 5-7 on pupils' worksheet 'Composing a Tango'

Main - composing

- Pupils compose their melodies by creating a one- or two-bar rhythmic motif, give it melodic shape (in keeping with the underlying chord sequence)
- Pupils develop the motif throughout the piece
- Finishing touches (dynamics, tempo, title and composer)

Plenary - listening

- Class listens to completed tangos
- Teacher prints out completed work

Latin Music: Assessment Sheet

CLASS ___ Name	Listening *Samba* — Identifies War Box / Identifies Repinique / Identifies Cuíca / Identifies Chocalho / Identifies Tambourine	Performing *Por una Cabeza* — Plays or sings dotted rhythms or triplets / Plays or sings a pitched part (not just rhythm) / Keeps timing and balance within / Plays two parts or elaborates on melody / Plays or sings with style and confidence	Composing *Tango* — Dotted rhythms in bass line and/or / Root position and first inversion chords / Parts playable on chosen instrumnets / Melody based on chord notes and motifs / Tempo, dynamic and other markings	Comments

173

Picture credits

Title page
Samba dancer No attribution required, Creative Commons Licence
https://pxhere.com/en/photo/472277

Listening to a Samba
Repinique Alno, Creative Commons Licence https://commons.wikimedia.org/wiki/File:Repique.JPG
Cuíca Alno, Creative Commons Licence https://commons.wikimedia.org/wiki/File:Cuica-fond.JPG
Caixa de Guerra Alno, Creative Commons Licence
https://commons.wikimedia.org/wiki/File:CaixaDeSamba.JPG
Tamborim Alno, Creative Commons Licence
https://commons.wikimedia.org/wiki/File:Tamborim.JPG
Surdo Alno, Creative Commons Licence
https://commons.wikimedia.org/wiki/File:Surdo22animal.JPG
Chocalho Alno, Creative Commons Licence https://pt.wikipedia.org/wiki/Ficheiro:Chocalho.JPG

Tango
'Por una cabeza' by Carlos Gardel (1890-1935), Public Domain, typeset by author
Bandoneon Pavel Krok, Creative Commons Licence
https://commons.wikimedia.org/wiki/File:Bandoneon-curved.jpg
Tango no attribution required, Creative Commons Licence https://pixabay.com/en/latin-dance-tango-ballroom-929817/

Romantic Music

KS3 Scheme of Work – 6-8 lessons

Objectives

- To listen to music, particularly waltzes, in different genres by composers from the Romantic era (1830-1900)
- To perform the accompaniment for a waltz on the keyboard
- To compose a 16-bar waltz for piano, fitting the melody to chosen four-bar chord sequences

Lesson Overview

- **Lesson 1: Romantic Music**
- **Lesson 2: Oom-pah-pah**
- **Lesson 3: A piano waltz**
- **Lesson 4: An orchestral waltz**
- **Lesson 5: An operatic waltz**
- Lesson 6: Listening to Programme Music
- Lessons 7/8: Composing Programme Music

Subject-specific vocabulary

- Instruments of the symphony orchestra: violins, viola, 'cello, double bass, harp, piccolo, flute, oboe, cor anglais, clarinet, bassoon, contrabassoon, horn, trumpet, trombone, tuba, percussion
- Romantic Composers: Chopin, Tchaikovsky, Johann Strauss jr, Grieg, Schubert, Berlioz, Wagner, Verdi
- Musical Genres: piano music, orchestral music, ballet, opera

Assessments

- Listening – Romantic Music (Lesson 1)
- Performing (keyboard) – 'Oom-pah-pah' accompaniment (Lesson 2)
- Composing – 16-bar waltz (Lessons 3-6)

Lesson 1: Romantic Music

Objectives

- To learn about the musical features of Romantic Music
- To apply this knowledge when listening to a Tchaikovsky overture

Resources

- Pupils' worksheets:
    - 'Romantic Music'
    - 'Listening to Romantic Music'
- YouTube clips:
    - Scene from *Swan Lake* by Tchaikovsky https://youtu.be/jSyZXfoS-YY
    - Ride of the Valkyries by Wagner (orchestral version) https://youtu.be/GGU1P6lBW6Q
    - The Beautiful Blue Danube by Johann Strauss Jr https://youtu.be/_CTYymbbEL4
    - 1812 Overture (finale) by Tchaikovsky https://youtu.be/u2W1Wi2U9sQ

Procedure

Starter - listening

- Pupils listen to three famous pieces from the Romantic Era (1830-1920)
- Pupils match up their composers and nationalities:
    - Scene from *Swan Lake* by Piotr Tchaikovsky (Russian)
    - Ride of the Valkyries from *The Valkyrie* by Richard Wagner (German)
    - The Beautiful Blue Danube by Johann Strauss Jr (Austrian)
- Pupils learn about the characteristics of Romantic Music at the bottom of the worksheet

Main - listening

- Pupils listen to the finale of the 1812 Overture three times and answer questions on the worksheet 'Listening to Romantic Music'

Plenary - appraising

- Teacher goes over the answers:
    1. French horns
    2. Violins
    3. Soft
    4. Louder
    5. Faster
    6. Slower
    7. Strings
    8. Brass
    9. Bells
    10. Cymbals

- Teacher records marks on Assessment Sheet:
    - Identifies specific groups of instruments (qus 1-2)
    - Identifies changes in dynamics (qu 3-4)
    - Identifies changes in tempo (qus 5-6)
    - Identifies families of instruments (qus 7-8)
    - Identifies specific percussion instruments (qus 9-10)

Lesson 2: Oom-pah-pah

Objective

- To learn about the 'oom-pah-pah' feel of the waltz through singing and playing the keyboard

Resources

- Lyrics for 'Oom-pah-pah' http://www.lyricsmode.com/lyrics/o/oliver/oom_pah_pah.html
- Pupils' worksheet: 'Oom-pah-pah'
- Keyboards and headphones

Procedure

Starter: singing

- Pupils learn to sing 'Oom-pah-pah' from lyrics on board

Main: performing on keyboard

- Pupils watch demonstration of chords and how to play them in 'oom-pah-pah' pattern
- Pupils draw a dot for each of the three notes of each chord on the keyboard diagrams
- Pupils practise playing the accompaniment on keyboard, differentiating as follows:
    - Basic level: play the bass line only (i.e. just the 'oom' of 'oom-pah-pah')
    - Standard level: play the bass line and chords with two hands
    - Advanced level: play the accompaniment in the left hand and the melody in the right hand

Plenary

- Pupils perform their waltz in front of the class

Lesson 3: The 'Minute' waltz

Objective
- To develop understanding of the 'oom-pah-pah' accompaniment by listening to and composing the accompaniment for a piano waltz from the Romantic Era

Resources
- Pupils' worksheets:
    - 'Chopin's Minute Waltz'
    - 'Composing a Waltz' (2 pages)
- Recording of The 'Minute' waltz by Chopin:
  https://www.youtube.com/watch?v=X2JCxapd5hU
- Keyboards and headphones (for composing)
- Laptops (if using music notation software to compose waltz)

N.B. The waltz can either be composed using music notation software or using handwritten notation.

Procedure

Starter: Listening
- Find out about the composer Chopin from handout
- Listen to Chopin's 'Minute' Waltz. Why do you think it is called the 'Minute' Waltz? (It has a quick tempo which means it does not last very long – although it's unlikely to be as short as one minute! Despite the title, the piece usually takes almost two minutes to play.)
- Look at the beginning of the score of Chopin's 'Minute' Waltz and observe:-
    - the tempo marking 'Molto vivace' (very lively)
    - the energetic melody, mainly made up of quavers (half-beat notes)
    - the pedal (Ped.) markings
    - the 'hairpins' showing where the music gets louder and quieter
    - the 'oom-pah-pah' accompaniment which splits the bass note and the chords

Main: Composing
- Play through given chord sequences on 'Composing a Waltz' worksheet and choose one for the first four bars and one for the next four bars. This composition will be developed next lesson.
- Compose a left-hand accompaniment, similar to Chopin's in his 'Minute' waltz, based on the chord sequence chosen last week (either on music notation software or by writing on the worksheet)

Plenary: Performing
- Some pupils play their 'oom-pah-pah' accompaniment to the class

Lesson 4: A symphonic waltz

Objective
- To develop understanding of the Romantic Era by listening to an orchestral symphonic movement

Resources
- Pupils' worksheets:
    - 'Composing a Waltz' (2 pages, from last lesson)
    - 'A Symphonic Waltz'
- Recording of 'Un bal' from *Symphonie Fantastique* by Berlioz: https://www.youtube.com/watch?v=s5HFufPG31g
- Keyboards and headphones (for composing)
- Laptops (if using music notation software to compose waltz)

Procedure

Starter: Listening
- Find out about the composer Berlioz and Romantic Orchestra from worksheet
- Listen to the first two minutes or so of 'A ball' from *Symphonie Fantastique* by Berlioz and answer the questions below:
    - Which family of instruments begins the piece? STRINGS
    - Which instrument plays arpeggios during the introduction (in fact, the word 'arpeggio' comes from the name of the instrument)? HARPS
    - What kind of dance is heard at the ball? WALTZ
    - Which instrument plays the main tune? VIOLIN(S)
    - Which family of instruments plays an upwards scale between tunes? WOODWIND

Main: Composing
- Compose a right-hand melody based on the chord sequence (either on music notation software or by writing on the worksheet)

Plenary: Performing
- Some pupils play their melody, with or without accompaniment, to the class

Lesson 5: An operatic waltz

Objective
- To broaden experience of Romantic music by listening to a waltz from an opera

Resources
- Pupils' worksheet: 'An Operatic Waltz'
- Video clip of 'Brindisi' from *La Traviata* with English subtitles:
  https://www.youtube.com/watch?v=UZvgmpiQCcI2

Procedure

Starter: Listening
- Pupils read about Verdi's opera *La Traviata*
- Listen to 'Brindisi' from *La Traviata* by the composer Verdi.
- Answer the questions below:
  1. What is the tempo of this waltz? FAST
  2. What is the voice-type of Alfredo, who begins the singing? TENOR
  3. Who sings the refrain at the end of the first verse? CHORUS
  4. What is the voice-type of Violetta, who sings the second verse? SOPRANO
  5. What is the name of a song like this for two singers? DUET

Main: Composing
- Pupils complete waltz composition. If they have enough time when they finish the melody, they can add tempo, dynamics, phrasing, pedalling and other performance directions

Plenary: Appraising
- Teacher plays some or all of the pupils' waltzes to the class
- Teacher assesses waltz composition (which does not need to be performed) using the criteria on the assessment sheet:
  - Correctly notates given chords
  - Splits chord into an oom-pah-pah pattern
  - Melody (mostly) fits the chords
  - Composes a waltz of 8 bars or more
  - Composes a waltz of 12 bars or more

Lesson 6: Listening to Programme Music

Objective

- To learn about Programme Music and Nationalism in nineteenth century music
- To listen to a complete tone poem, noting musical features and how they portray the 'story' of the programme music

Resources

- Pupils' worksheets:
    - 'Programme Music' (2 pages)
- YouTube clip of Smetana's Vltava: https://youtu.be/kdtLuyWuPDs

Procedure

Starter

- Read introduction to Programme Music, Nationalism and Smetana's 'Vltava'

Main - listening

- Listen to Smetana's Vltava, indicating sections (A-H) as they begin:
    A. The spring that is the source of the river [0.00]
    B. The river flowing through the mountains [0.53]
    C. Passing some hunters in the forest [1.53]
    D. Passing a village wedding [2.43]
    E. The mermaids come out at night [4.10]
    F. The river continues on its way [6.30]
    G. The river goes through rapids [7.17]
    H. The river triumphantly enters the capital city [8.28]

Plenary - appraising

- Teacher goes through answers with pupils:
    1. Czech Republic
    2. Smetana went deaf
    3. Flutes
    4. Violins
    5. (French) horn
    6. Polka
    7. High
    8. Minor
    9. Cymbals
    10. Major

Lessons 7/8 - Composing Programme Music

- One or two more lessons can be spent composing programme music on computers, keyboards or other instruments

Romantic Music: Assessment Sheet

CLASS ___ / Name	Listening — *1812 Overture*	Performing — *Oom-pah-pah*	Composing — *Waltz for Piano*	Comments
	Identifies specific groups of instruments / Identifies changes in dynamics (qu 3-4) / Identifies changes in tempo (qus 5-6) / Identifies families of instruments (qus 7-) / Identifies specific percussion instruments	Plays with a steady pulse of three beats in / Plays a single bass note on the first beat of / Plays chord on the second and third beats / Performs with style and confidence / Sings melody OR plays in right hand	Correctly notates given chords / Splits chord into an oom-pah-pah pattern / Melody (mostly) fits the chords / Composes a waltz of 8 bars or more / Composes a waltz of 12 bars or more	

183

Picture credits

Title page
Cheney, Harriet (1771-1848): The Upper Part of Ulswater from Lyulph's Tower., The Wordsworth Trust, Dove Cottage, Grasmere, UK, Public Domain http://www.amdigital.co.uk/m-products/product/romanticism-life-literature-and-landscape/

Romantic Music
Swan Lake nikidinov, Creative Commons Licence https://pixabay.com/en/ballet-swan-lake-ballerina-dance-2124651/
Valkyrie Public Domain https://commons.wikimedia.org/wiki/File:Rhinegold_and_the_Valkyries_p_122.jpg
Waltz Susanlenox, no copyright https://www.flickr.com/photos/jumborois/3188893874/sizes/o/
Flag-map of Russia Public Domain https://commons.wikimedia.org/wiki/File:Flag-map_of_Russia.svg
Flag-map of Austria Public Domain https://commons.wikimedia.org/wiki/File:Flag-map_of_Austria.svg
Flag-map of Germany Public Domain https://commons.wikimedia.org/wiki/File:Flag_map_of_Germany.svg
Composers contemporary portraits, Public Domain

The Waltz
Couple waltzing Public Domain https://commons.wikimedia.org/wiki/File:Man_and_woman_dancing_a_waltz_(1887).gif
Keyboard diagram ivinx110, Creative Commons Licence https://pixabay.com/en/piano-keyboard-instrument-847409/

Chopin's 'Minute' Waltz
Chopin contemporary portrait, Public Domain

A Symphonic Waltz
Berlioz contemporary portrait, Public Domain
Orchestra diagram Ho3ein33, Creative Commons Licence (image modified under terms of licence) https://commons.wikimedia.org/wiki/File:Orchestra-a.jpg

An Operatic Waltz
Verdi contemporary portrait, Public Domain
La Traviata © Heritage Opera, used with permission

Programme Music
Smetana contemporary portrait, Public Domain
Excerpts from 'Vltava' Public Domain, typeset by author

Gospel, Blues and Soul

KS3 Scheme of Work – (6-8 lessons)

Objectives

- To learn about the evolution of African-American styles in the 1950s and 1960s
- To listen to examples of spirituals, gospel, rhythm and blues, and soul
- To consolidate previous knowledge of major and minor chords
- To learn how to play seventh chords
- To sing songs from these styles, both in class and individually
- To arrange and perform these styles as a group

Lesson Overview

1. Two Spirituals
2. Gospel Music
3. Rhythm 'n' Blues
4. The Birth of Soul
5. Respect
6. Stand By Me
7. Group arrangement*
8. Group performance*

* The group arrangement/performance forms an optional extension task

Subject-specific vocabulary

- Primary triads – I, IV, V
- Triads – C, F, G, Am, D, E
- Seventh chords
- Call-and-response
- Ornamentation
- Improvisation

Assessments

- Performing – chord sequences for various songs on keyboard (Lessons 1, 5, 6)
- Listening – 'The Birth of Soul' (Lesson 4)
- Composing (arranging) – chosen song in a small ensemble (Lessons 7-8)

Lesson 1 – Two Spirituals

Objectives

- To sing two spirituals, both separately and together
- To play the accompaniment for these spirituals using primary triads (I, IV and V)
- To learn that spirituals were African American religious songs at the turn of the twentieth century

Resources

- Pupils' worksheets:
    - 'Two Spirituals'
    - 'Primary Triads'
- Chordal instruments: keyboards, pianos, guitars, ukuleles

Procedure

Starter – performing

- Pupils learn to sing 'Swing Low, Sweet Chariot' and 'When the Saints Go Marching In' from the worksheet 'Two Spirituals' (both in key of C major – 'Swing Low' starts on E and 'When the Saints' starts on C)
- Pupils divide into two groups and sing the two songs together – the group singing 'Swing Low, Sweet Chariot' ait for three notes of 'When the Saints' before you start 'Swing Low'

Main – performing

- On the worksheet 'Primary Triads', pupils work out the name of chords iv (four) and v (five)
- Pupils write a dot on the three notes in each chord, then write down letter-names for the three notes
- Pupils learn/revise the chords C, F and G on the keyboard, mostly in pairs:
    - Less able pupils play the bass note (root of the chord) on the left-hand side of the keyboard
    - Most pupils play the three-note chord on the left- or right-hand side of the keyboard
    - More able pupils play the bass notes in the left hand and the chords in the right hand
- When the class can form the chords/bass notes, they should learn the chord sequence at the bottom of the worksheet
- Extension task for more able pupils: play the same chord sequence in different keys (e.g. D major)

Plenary – performing

- Depending on time and inclination, some or all pupils play the chord sequence in front of the class, optionally with the rest of the class singing one or both spirituals
- Where pupils have met any of the performing assessment criteria, the teacher records the skills demonstrated on the assessment sheet (there will be further opportunities to assess pupils' performance):
    - Plays roots of primary triads
    - Forms primary triads (three-note chords)

- Forms seventh chords [not applicable in this performance]
- Plays with sense of pulse
- Plays bass in left hand and chords in right hand Plays bass in left hand and chords in right hand

Lesson 2: Gospel Music

Objectives
- To listen to and sing a gospel song, noting its musical features
- To sing or play the call-and-response/accompaniment to the gospel song
- To apply this knowledge when listening to another gospel song

Resources
- Pupils' worksheets:
    - 'O Happy Day'
    - 'Gospel Music'
- YouTube video of original hymn 'O Happy Day': https://youtu.be/_uLxtajmyRI
- YouTube video of gospel song 'O Happy Day': https://youtu.be/ihGHltBuBBI
- Sheet music for 'O Happy Day': http://www.jarcher.co.uk/vocaleyes/O%20Happy%20Day.pdf
- Chordal instruments: keyboards, pianos, guitars, ukuleles
- YouTube video of another Gospel song: Kathy Taylor- "Oh How Precious," Mt Zion Nashville https://youtu.be/wO35mZ1mneM

Procedure

Starter – listening
- Listen to two versions of 'O Happy Day': the original hymn (with words dating from the eighteenth century and music from the nineteenth) and the gospel version (arranged in the twentieth century)
- What are the differences between these two versions?
    - The original hymn is sung in unison with a homophonic accompaniment, whereas in the gospel version there is a regular call-and-response pattern between the soloists and the choir, singing in harmony
    - The original hymn is accompanied by a piano, whereas the gospel version is accompanied by several instruments, including drum kit, electric guitar and bass guitar (and handclaps)
    - In the original hymn, the congregation sings the composed melody, whereas in the gospel version, the soloists embellish the melody with improvisation
    - The original hymn uses a repeated verse-chorus structure, whereas the gospel version uses ternary form (outer sections sung by a male soloist, middle by a female) with an extended coda (sung by both)

Main – performing
- Teacher teaches pupils the main melody of 'O Happy Day' in the gospel version from the sheet music, accompanying them on a chordal instrument (keyboard, piano, guitar, or ukulele)
- Pupils learn the chord sequence on a chordal instrument (keyboard, piano, guitar, or ukulele)
- If pupils are working on pianos or keyboards, they can work as follows:
    - Less able pupils play the bass note (root of the chord) on the left-hand side of the keyboard
    - Most pupils play the three-note chord on the left- or right-hand side of the keyboard

- More able pupils play the bass notes in the left hand and the chords in the right hand

Plenary – appraising/listening

- Read about gospel and write response to another gospel song on the worksheet 'Gospel'

Lesson 3: Rhythm 'n' Blues

Objectives
- To listen to two examples of 1950s Rhythm 'n' Blues songs and note their musical features
- To play a Rhythm 'n' Blues song using the 12-bar blues chord sequence in a small ensemble

Resources
- Pupils' worksheets:
    - 'Rhythm 'n' Blues'
    - 'Shake, Rattle 'n' Roll'
- YouTube videos of two 1950s Rhythm 'n' Blues performances, plus a Rock 'n' Roll performance for comparison:
    - Ruth Brown – Mama, He Treats Your Daughter Mean (1953)
      https://www.youtube.com/watch?v=2WKxJfmN_ac
    - Big Joe Turner - *Shake, Rattle & Roll* (1954)
      https://www.youtube.com/watch?v=20Feq_Nt3nM
    - Bill Haley and the Comets - *Shake, Rattle & Roll* (1954)
      https://youtu.be/FqSIvwZVFoQ
- Instruments for small ensembles, depending on availability and pupils' own instruments, e.g.:
    - Keyboards
    - Guitars
    - Percussion instruments

Procedure

Starter (listening)
- Pupils listen to two examples of 1950s R&B: plus a Rock 'n' Roll performance for comparison:
    - Ruth Brown – Mama, He Treats Your Daughter Mean (1953)
    - Big Joe Turner - *Shake, Rattle & Roll* (1954)
    - Bill Haley and the Comets - *Shake, Rattle & Roll* (1954)
- Pupils read through the worksheet 'Rhythm 'n' Blues'
- Pupils discuss the musical features of Rhythm 'n' Blues and note them down at the bottom of the worksheet

Main (performing)
- Recap on chords C, F and G and 12-bar blues sequence.

Plenary
- Group performs to class

Lesson 4: The Birth of Soul

Objectives
- To understand how Soul Music evolved as a fusion between Gospel (sacred music) and Rhythm 'n' Blues (secular music)

Resources
- YouTube clip of scene from *The Color Purple*: https://youtu.be/9Z8WRdGIZoU
- YouTube ½ hour edited version of BBC's 'Soul Deep – Episode 1': https://vimeo.com/232027164
- Pupils' two-sided worksheet 'The Birth of Soul'

Procedure

Starter – listening
- Pupils watch the scene from *The Color Purple* (1985) where Shug Avery, a pastor's daughter who has gone astray, leads her audience from the jook joint (drinking and gambling establishment) to the church
- What two styles of music are heard in this clip? (Rhythm 'n' Blues and Gospel.)
- Teacher explains that these two styles of African American music – one secular, one sacred – were brought together in the late 1950s to make soul music

Main – appraising
- Pupils watch ½ hour edited version of BBC's 'Soul Deep – Episode 1'
- Pupils answer questions on two-sided worksheet 'The Birth of Soul'

Plenary – appraising
- Teacher goes over answers for the worksheet 'The Birth of Soul':

1. D	2. B	3. A	4. E	5. A	6. C	7. A
8. B	9. B	10. D	11. D	12. C	13. E	

- Up to two marks can be awarded for question 14 – whatever each pupil's preference, credit is given for accurately describing a musical element they like about the style
- For example, 'I like Soul Music because of it combines vocal harmonies with electric guitar and drum kit' would receive 2 marks
- Teacher records marks as the main listening/appraising assessment

Lesson 5: Respect

Objectives
- To compare two versions of the same soul song
- To learn about the formation of seventh chords
- To perform a soul song as a class (singing and accompanying)

Resources
- YouTube clips of two soul singers' performances of the song 'Respect':
    - Otis Redding https://youtu.be/KvC9V_lBnDQ
    - Aretha Franklin https://youtu.be/6FOUqQt3Kg0
- Pupils' worksheets:
    - 'Seventh chords'
    - 'Respect'
- Lyrics for Aretha Franklin's 'Respect':
  https://play.google.com/music/preview/Twnsdqfbn5js5s76c2s2pvw2h3m
- Keyboards

Procedure

Starter - listening
- Pupils listen to Otis Redding and Aretha Franklin singing 'Respect'
- Pupils answer questions orally, recapping on previous lesson:
    - What two styles of African American music do these songs combine? (Gospel and rhythm 'n' blues – the sacred and the secular.)
    - How does it combine elements of gospel and rhythm 'n' blues? (Vocal harmonies and use of Hammond organ from gospel music; electric guitar, electric bass and drum kit from R 'n' B).
    - How do the lyrics of this song capture the political climate of the 1960s? (Civil rights and feminist movements – demanding equal rights for all)
- Pupils compare the two versions on the worksheet 'Respect'

Main - performing
- Learn to sing 'Respect' from lyrics (verse and chorus only – middle eight is instrumental)
- Learn how to form seventh chords on the worksheet 'Seventh chords'
- Learn to play the chord sequence for 'Respect' on the keyboard using seventh chords
- Teacher can give credit on the Assessment Sheet (performing) to those pupils who are able to form seventh chords

Plenary
- Class performs 'Respect' by singing and/or playing the chord sequence on the keyboard

Lesson 6: Stand By Me

Objectives
- To learn how to sing and play a soul song using the I-vi-IV-V chord progression

Resources
- YouTube clip of Ben E. King singing 'Stand By Me': https://youtu.be/hwZNL7QVJjE
- Pupils' worksheets:
    - 'The I-vi-IV-V progression'
    - 'Stand By Me'

Procedure

Starter - listening
- Pupils listen to Ben E. King singing 'Stand By Me'
- Can you hear any **ostinato** (repeating patterns)?
- Answer: 8-bar bass/chord ostinato (and 1-bar guiro/triangle ostinato)

Main - performing
- Learn to sing 'Stand By Me' in C as a class, by copying one phrase at a time demonstrated the teacher
- Learn to sing bass ostinato to 'doo-doo-doo' etc.
- Combine melody and bass ostinato in 2 parts
- Complete the chord diagrams on the worksheet 'The I-vi-IV-V progression'
- Learn chord sequence in C on keyboard (C, Am, F, G)
- (EXT) learn bass ostinato on keyboard

Plenary – performing
- Perform 'Stand By Me' as a class, combining the sung melody with the I-iv-IV-V chord sequence and bass ostinato

Lessons 7-8 – Group arrangement/performance

Objective
- To arrange one of the songs learnt during the topic for a group performance, with different pupils singing or playing instruments

Resources
- Pupils' worksheets on the following songs:
    - 'Two Spirituals'
    - 'O Happy Day'
    - 'Shake, Rattle and Roll'
    - 'Respect'
    - 'Stand By Me'

Procedure

Starter (appraising)
- Teacher explains that the class is going to split into several groups, each group concentrating on one of the songs studied so far in the topic:
    - 'Two Spirituals' – would suit lower ability pupils, as the melody and rhythms are straightforward
    - 'O Happy Day' – would particularly suit a predominantly vocal group that can arrange the call-and-response in two- or three-part harmony
    - 'Shake, Rattle and Roll' – would suit a predominantly instrumental group who would like to play a 12-bar blues in 1950s rhythm 'n' blues style
    - 'Respect' – would particularly suit a predominantly vocal group that can arrange the call-and-response in harmony
    - 'Stand By Me' – would suit a mixed ability group, as the percussion ostinati are simple, but the syncopated bass line is more challenging, especially when played together with the chordal rhythm on a piano or keyboard

Main - arranging
- Pupils arrange and practise their chosen song as a group, for example:
    - One or more pupils play percussion parts on a drum kit or other unpitched percussion instruments
    - One (very able) pupil plays hands together on keyboard (chords and bass) OR one (fairly able) pupil plays chords and another (less able) pupil plays bass ostinato on keyboard (all of these parts are more challenging if they involve a syncopated rhythm, as in 'Stand By Me')
    - One pupil plays bass line on the keyboard, piano, double bass or cello
    - One pupil plays chords on keyboard, guitar or ukulele
    - One or more pupils sings the solo melody
    - Two or more pupils sing the choral responses
- Teacher guides and supervises the groups as they are practising

Plenary - performing
- The groups perform their chosen songs to the rest of the class
- Teacher assesses the pupils' Composing (arranging) skills on the Assessment Sheet

Gospel, Blues and Soul: Assessment Sheet

CLASS ___ / Name	Performing — Chords (keyboard): Plays roots of primary triads	Forms primary triads (three-note chords)	Forms seventh chords	Plays with sense of pulse	Plays bass in left hand and chords in right	Listening — The Birth of Soul: Origins of soul music (qus 1-3)	Origins of Rhythm & Blues (qus 4-6)	Development of Rhythm & Blues (qus 7-)	Origins of soul (qu 10-13)	Expresses/justifies musical preferences	Arranging — Song for small ensemble: Maintains sense of pulse	Rhythmic variety in part	Listens to others in group	Plays different pitches (or percussion)	Performs with confidence and style	Comments

Picture credits

Cover page
Soul group Public Domain
https://commons.wikimedia.org/wiki/File:The_Stylistics_on_Soul_Train_1974.jpg

Primary Triads
Hands on keyboard No attribution required, Creative Commons licence https://pixabay.com/p-1481408/?no_redirect

Gospel
Gospel choir Maryland Slater, Creative Commons licence
https://commons.wikimedia.org/wiki/File:Morgan_State_University_Choir.jpg

Rhythm 'n' Blues
Big Joe Turner Public Domain
https://commons.wikimedia.org/wiki/File:Big_Joe_Turner_Rock_and_Roll_Revue_Apollo_Theater_1955.jpg
Ruth Brown caviera, Creative Commons licence
https://commons.wikimedia.org/wiki/File:Ruth_Brown_cropped.jpg

The Birth of Soul
Ray Charles William Morris Agency (management)/Photo by Maurice Seymour, New York, Public Domain https://commons.wikimedia.org/wiki/File:Ray_Charles_classic_piano_pose.jpg

Respect
Otis Redding Public Domain https://commons.wikimedia.org/wiki/File:Otis_Redding_(2).png
Aretha Franklin Public Domain https://commons.wikimedia.org/wiki/File:Aretha_Franklin.png

Stand By Me
Guiro grace_kat, Creative Commons Licence
https://www.flickr.com/photos/g_kat26/3496826512/sizes/m/in/photostream/
Triangle Precision, Public Domain
https://commons.wikimedia.org/wiki/File:Triangel_(Instrument).png

Printed in Great Britain
by Amazon